❋ ❘ ❋ ❘ ❋ ❘ ❋ ❘ ❋ ❘ ❋ ❘ ❋ ❘ ❋ ❘ ❋ ❘ ❋ ❘ ❋ ❘ ❋ ❘ ❋

DEFEAT
DEPRESSION
THE CBT WAY

Cognitive Behavioral Therapy methods to undo Depression and it's effects

❋ ❘ ❋ ❘ ❋ ❘ ❋ ❘ ❋ ❘ ❋ ❘ ❋ ❘ ❋ ❘ ❋ ❘ ❋ ❘ ❋ ❘ ❋ ❘ ❋

Cathrine Kowal

Table of Contents

Chapter 1

Introduction

The Problem of Depression

According to some authoritative sources, at least 12% of the adult population is prone to episodic but quite pronounced depression and therefore requires treatment for depressive disorders. Over the past 15 years, hundreds of systematic studies have been carried out related to the biological substrate of depression and the pharmacotherapy of depression. Various publications, both from government sources and from the private sector, argue that there has been a breakthrough in understanding the psychobiology of depression and treating this disorder with medication.

However, this generally rainbow-colored picture is confusing for clinicians. Despite significant advances in the pharmacotherapy of depression, the disease is still widespread. Moreover, the number of suicides, which is considered to be an indicator of the prevalence of depression, has not just decreased but increased in recent years. The sustainability of this indicator seems especially significant, given the enormous impact that the efforts to create and support suicide prevention centers across the country have brought.

A special report by the National Institute of Mental Health "Depressive Disorders" states that 75% of all psychiatric hospitalizations are associated with depression and that 15% of adults aged 18 to 74 years experience symptoms of depression. In monetary terms, this state of affairs is estimated by the authors in the range from 3 million to 9 million dollars. And these same authors emphasize that "The main burden of therapy for depressive disorders (75% of all psychiatric hospitalizations) rests with psychosocial therapeutic modalities."

The Importance of Psychotherapy in the Treatment of Depression

The value of effective psychotherapy for the treatment of depression is self-evident, and we see our task in clearly defining the indications and contraindications for its use, as well as in establishing its role in the overall treatment of a depressed patient. Since psychotherapy is used to some extent and in various forms in the treatment of almost all depressed patients, it is extremely important to define specific forms of psychotherapy and evaluate their effectiveness so that the consumer knows whether this expensive service brings beneficial results. However, there are other reasons for identifying and testing specific psychotherapeutic modalities.

1. It is clear that drug treatment is much cheaper than psychotherapy, but not all depressed patients respond to antidepressants. According to the most optimistic estimates, based on the results of numerous controlled studies in the field

of pharmacotherapy for depression, only 60-65% of patients show a pronounced improvement as a result of using conventional tricyclic drugs (see Beck, 1973, p. 86). Therefore, for 35-40% of depressed patients who did not benefit from drug treatment, other methods should be used.

2. Many of the patients who could benefit from medication either refuse to take the medication for personal reasons, or stop the course because of side effects.

3. In the long run, drug dependence can indirectly affect the patient's ability to use their own psychological methods to overcome depression. The extensive literature on the problem of "attribution" suggests that patients taking drugs usually look for the cause of their problems in chemical imbalances and explain their improvement only by the action of drugs. As a result, as shown by socio-psychological studies, the patient is no longer particularly inclined to engage or develop their own coping mechanisms with depression. A relatively high percentage of patients who previously underwent medical treatment (approximately 50% the next year after the end of therapy) can confirm the above assumption.

Simple common sense tells us that an effective course of psychotherapy in the long term can be more beneficial than pharmacotherapy since psychotherapeutic experience is of educational value to the patient. The patient develops effective ways to overcome depression, learns to recognize its approach and take the necessary measures, and possibly even prevent depression.

The fact that the number of suicides is still high despite the extremely widespread use of antidepressants indicates that pharmacotherapy, although it serves as a temporary solution to the suicidal crisis, does not protect the patient from attempting suicide in the future. Studies show that the psychological core of a suicidal patient is a sense of hopelessness (or "generalized negative expectations"). The positive results of work with a sense of hopelessness in depressed patients convince us that cognitive therapy has a more stable "anti-suicidal effect" compared to pharmacotherapy.

Definition of Cognitive Therapy

Cognitive therapy is an active, prescriptive, time-limited, structured approach used in the treatment of various psychiatric disorders (e.g., depression, anxiety, phobias, pain, etc.). This approach is based on a theoretical premise according to which a person's emotions and behavior are largely determined by how he structures the world. Man's ideas (verbal or figurative "events" present in his mind) are determined by his attitudes and mental constructions (patterns) formed as a result of past experience. For example, in the thinking of a person who interprets an event in terms of his own competence or adequacy, such a scheme may dominate: "Until I achieve perfection in everything, I am a failure." This scheme determines his reaction to a variety of situations, even those that have nothing to do with his competence.

The therapeutic techniques used in this approach are based on a cognitive model of psychopathology; we are convinced that therapy cannot be effective without a sound theoretical foundation. These techniques make it possible to identify, analyze, and correct erroneous conceptualizations and dysfunctional beliefs (schemes) of the patient. The patient learns to solve problems and find solutions to situations that previously seemed insurmountable to him, rethinking them and correcting his thinking. A cognitive therapist helps the patient think and act more realistically and adaptively, and thereby eliminates the symptoms that concern him.

Cognitive therapy uses a variety of cognitive and behavioral strategies. Cognitive techniques are aimed at identifying and testing erroneous ideas and maladaptive mindsets. During therapy, the patient learns to perform highly specific operations, namely: 1) to track his negative automatic thoughts (ideas); 2) recognize the relationship between their own thoughts, emotions, and behavior; 3) to analyze the facts confirming or refuting his views; 4) develop more realistic assessments and perceptions; 5) to identify and modify dysfunctional beliefs predisposing him to a distortion of experience.

Various verbal techniques are used in order to understand what logic is hiding behind certain representations and mental constructions of the patient. First, the patient has explained the mechanisms of cognitive therapy, after which they are taught to recognize, track, and record their negative thoughts in a special "Daily Record of Dysfunctional Thoughts." Then the patient, together with the therapist, analyzes the recorded thoughts and experiences in order to establish the degree of their logic, validity, and adaptability and outline positive patterns of behavior instead of pathological ones. Thus, for example, the patient's tendency to take responsibility for any negative results and inability to recognize his own achievements are analyzed. Therapy focuses on specific "target symptoms" (e.g., suicidal impulses). We establish and then subject to logical and empirical testing the thoughts and beliefs that nourish these symptoms (for example: "My life is meaningless, and I cannot change anything"). One of the powerful components of the educational model of psychotherapy is that the patient gradually adopts many therapeutic techniques from the therapist. At some point, he suddenly discovers that he begins to play the role of a therapist in relation to himself, casting doubt on his own conclusions or predictions. Here are just some examples of self-inquiry that we happened to observe: What facts is my conclusion based on? Are other explanations possible? How serious is this loss? Does she take anything really important from my life? What is wrong for me if an outsider thinks badly of me? What will I lose if I try to assert my rights more persistently?

This kind of self-inquiry is crucial for transferring cognitive techniques from the interview situation to everyday situations. It helps the patient free himself from the stereotyped automatic patterns of thinking - a phenomenon that can be called "thoughtless thinking."

Behavioral techniques are used in cases of severe depression, not only to change behavior but also to identify associated concepts. Since patients usually require the use of these more active techniques at the beginning of treatment, the material on behavioral strategies will precede the description of cognitive techniques.

Examples of behavioral strategies we use include: "Weekly schedule of activities," where the patient writes on the clock what he should do in a week, "Scale of skill and pleasure," by which he evaluates the fulfillment of the tasks presented in the schedule, and "Graduated tasks" when the patient is instructed to complete a series of tasks that bring him closer to a goal that seems unattainable to him. In addition, special behavioral tasks are developed to help the patient verify and revise their maladaptive ideas and ideas.

An important question facing the therapist is the question of what type of intervention and when should be applied when working with a particular patient. Both behavioral and cognitive techniques have their own merits and applications in cognitive therapy. It is extremely difficult for a retarded, completely absorbed in one idea patient to engage in introspection since he is not able to shift his attention from one to another. In fact, this procedure can even enhance his concern and perseverance, while the behavioral methods that mobilize the patient for constructive activity are quite powerful weapons in the fight against inertia. In addition, successful experience in achieving a specific behavioral goal can serve as a more convincing refutation of misconceptions such as "I am not capable of anything."

However, while behavioral tasks can more clearly refute the patient's erroneous beliefs, cognitive techniques may be the best type of intervention when it is necessary to correct the patient's incorrect conclusions regarding specific events. Imagine a patient who concluded that her friends did not like her because they had not called her in recent days. It is clear that in this case, it is necessary to check the "logical" processes leading the patient to such a conclusion, consider all the facts and work out alternative explanations. The behavioral assignment will not help solve this cognitive problem.

Without adherence to these principles, consistent therapy is not possible. The therapist, as you gain experience, can use the "decision tree" when conducting therapeutic interviews. Instead of choosing strategies at random, so to speak, pointing the finger at the sky, he chooses the technique that is most appropriate for a particular symptom or specific problem.

Typically, a course of cognitive therapy consists of 15-25 sessions, with weekly intervals between them. For patients with moderate to severe depression, interviews are usually conducted twice a week for a minimum of 4-5 weeks and then once a week for 10-15 weeks. The last meetings of the patient with the therapist as part of the regular course of therapy are usually held every two weeks, after which we recommend the patient "booster therapy." These additional meetings may be held on a regular basis or at the discretion of the patient. According to our observations, the average patient comes to the therapist 3-4 times a year after completing the official course of therapy.

New Features of Cognitive Therapy

What is new in this type of psychotherapy? Cognitive therapy differs from conventional forms of psychotherapy in two important aspects: the structure of the interview and the types of problems that are in its focus.

"Collaboration plus Empiricism." A feature of cognitive therapy that distinguishes it from more traditional types of psychotherapy, such as psychoanalysis and client-centered therapy, lies in the active position of the therapist and his constant desire to cooperate with the patient. The therapist designs the treatment in such a way as to encourage the patient to participate and collaborate. A depressed patient comes to the therapist confused, distracted, and lost in thought, and therefore, the therapist must first help him organize his thinking and behavior - without this, it is impossible to teach the patient how to cope with the requirements of everyday life. Due to the symptoms present at this stage, the patient often shies away from cooperation, and the therapist has to be resourceful and inventive in order to encourage the patient to participate in various therapeutic operations actively. We found that classical psychoanalytic techniques and techniques, such as the free association technique, involving a minimum of activity by the therapist, are not applicable when working with depressed patients, as the patient is even more immersed in the quagmire of his negative thoughts and ideas.

Unlike psychoanalytic therapy, the content of cognitive therapy is determined by the problems here and now. We do not attach much importance to the patient's childhood memories unless they help clarify current observations. The main thing for us is to research what the patient thinks and feels during the session and in between sessions. We do not interpret the unconscious. A cognitive therapist, actively interacting and collaborating with the patient, explores his psychological experiences, outlines a plan of action for the patient, and gives him homework.

Cognitive therapy is distinguished from behavioral therapy by greater attention to the internal (mental) experience, thoughts, feelings, desires, fantasies, and attitudes of the patient. In general, the strategy of cognitive therapy, which distinguishes it from all other therapeutic schools and directions, is an empirical study of "machine" thoughts, conclusions, and assumptions of the patient. Formulating dysfunctional beliefs and representations of the patient about himself, his own experience and his own future in the form of hypotheses, we then suggest that the patient use certain procedures to verify the reliability of these hypotheses. Almost any internal experience can be the starting point of an experiment to test the patient's negative beliefs or beliefs. For example, if the patient believes that others turn away from him with disgust, we help him develop a system of criteria for evaluating human reactions and then encourage him to evaluate gestures and facial expressions of people objectively. If the patient is convinced of his inability to perform the simplest hygienic procedures, the therapist can involve him in the preparation of a special form in which the patient will subsequently note how well or poorly he performs these procedures.

Cognitive Models: Historical Perspective

Cognitive therapy proceeds from the following general theoretical propositions.

- Perception and experience as a whole are active processes involving both objective and introspective data.

- Representations and ideas are the results of a synthesis of internal and external stimuli.

- Products of a person's cognitive activity (thoughts and images) make it possible to predict how he will evaluate a particular situation.

- Thoughts and images form a "stream of consciousness" or a phenomenal field, reflecting a person's ideas about himself, the world, his past, and the future.

- The deformation of the content of basic cognitive structures causes negative changes in the emotional state and behavior of a person.

- Psychological therapy can help the patient recognize cognitive impairment.

- By adjusting these distorted dysfunctional constructs, an improvement in the patient's condition can be achieved.

The origins of cognitive therapy are traced in the philosophy of the Stoics, in particular in the writings of Zeno from Kition (IV century BC), Chrysippus, Cicero, Seneca, Epictetus, and Marcus Aurelius. Epictetus wrote in his "Guide": "People are not upset by things, but by ideas about things." As in Stoicism, in Eastern philosophies, such as Taoism and Buddhism, it is emphasized that ideas are the basis of human emotions. A person can control even the strongest feelings if he changes his mind.

Freud (1900/1953) initially also believed that unconscious ideas underlie pathological symptoms and affect. Alfred Adler, in his work "Individual Psychology," emphasized that in order to understand the patient, one must turn to his conscious experiences. According to Adler, therapy is an attempt to trace how a person perceives and feels the world. Adler (1931/1958) wrote:

"We do not suffer from emotional upheavals - the so-called injuries, but we extract from them what is consistent with our goals. We are self-determined by the meaning that we attach to what happened to us, and there is probably something wrong with the fact that we put a separate experience at the heart of our future life. Not the values depend on the situations, but we depend on the values that we endow with the situations."

Many other authors who have left the school of psychoanalysis or experienced the influence of the psychoanalytic tradition have contributed to the development of cognitive psychotherapy. (A comprehensive review is contained in Raimy, 1975.) The most influential names in this series are Alexander (Alexander, 1950), Horney (Horney, 1950), Saul (Saul, 1947), and Sullivan (1953).

The philosophical emphasis on conscious subjective experience originates from the work of Kant, Heidegger, and Husserl. This "phenomenological movement" had a significant impact on the development of modern psychology and psychotherapy.

Recently, representatives of the behavioral approach have recognized the importance of cognitive formations in the regulation of human activity. Bauer (Bowers, 1973) advocated an interactive model of subject-environment relations and opposed the "situationism" of the classical behavioral school. A growing interest in cognitive restructuring formations, modifying cognitive processes is reflected in the work of Arnold Lazarus (1972), which states: "The bulk of psychotherapeutic efforts are now focused on correcting the patient's misconceptions." The latter, argues Lazarus, can both precede and follow behavioral changes in behavior.

A growing number of American psychotherapists write about how a therapist can systematically modify thinking and perception during psychotherapy. Based on his own theory of personality constructs, Kelly (Kelly, 1955) proposes to direct therapy to change the patient's conscious daily experiences. If in traditional therapy, where the roles are strictly separated, the patient is invited to proceed from ideas that do not coincide with his daily experiences, perception of the world and himself, then, taking on the role of the therapist, the patient is alone with his own ideas about yourself and your relationships with people. Kelly calls these representations "personality constructs."

Berne (Berne, 1961, 1964) and Frank (Frank, 1961) supplemented the therapy aimed at changing the patient's current conscious experience or cognitive formations with a number of new methods and concepts.

The work of Ellis (Ellis, 1957, 1962, 1971, 1973) became a powerful stimulus in the development of cognitive-behavioral forms of therapy. Ellis believes that the link between the environmental or activating event (AS) and the emotional consequences (EP) is a belief (Y). His rationally emotive psychotherapy aims to make the patient fully aware of his irrational beliefs and the harmful emotional consequences of these beliefs. Rational-emotive therapy aims to modify basic irrational beliefs. The possibility of using other techniques to familiarize the patient with his beliefs and their subsequent modification was demonstrated by Moltsby (Maultsby, 1975).

Recent studies of representatives of the behavioral school (Mahoney, 1974; Meichenbaum, 1977; Goldfried, Davison, 1976; Kazdin, Wilson, 1978) provided even more solid empirical and theoretical grounds for the development of therapy in this direction.

Cognitive therapy for depression consists of a number of interrelated techniques that have undergone rigorous clinical testing in working with depressed patients. These techniques are applied within the framework of a theory that explains the psychological structure of depression (Beck, 1976). As mentioned above, using cognitive therapy techniques is not possible without understanding the cognitive model of depression.

The Cognitive Model of Depression

The cognitive model of depression is the result of systematic clinical observations and experimental studies (Beck, 1963, 1964, 1967). It was a combination of clinical and experimental approaches that made it possible to build this theoretical model and formulate the principles of cognitive therapy.

The cognitive model contains three specific concepts that explain the psychological structure of depression: 1) the cognitive triad, 2) patterns, and 3) cognitive errors (incorrect processing of information).

The Concept of the Cognitive Triad

The cognitive triad is made up of three basic cognitive patterns that determine the patient's idiosyncratic attitude toward himself, his own future, and his current experience. The first component of the triad is associated with the negative attitude of the patient to his own person. The patient considers himself flawed, inadequate, terminally ill or deprived. He is inclined to explain his failures with the alleged psychological, moral, or physical defects. The patient is convinced that these imaginary defects made him a worthless, useless creature; he constantly blames and scolds himself for them. And finally, he believes that he is deprived of all that brings a person happiness and a sense of satisfaction.

The second component of the cognitive triad is the tendency to interpret your current experience negatively. It seems to the patient that the world around him imposes exorbitant demands on him and / or poses insurmountable obstacles to him on the way to achieving life goals. In any experience of interaction with the environment, he sees only defeat and loss. The tendentiousness and fallacy of these interpretations are especially evident when the patient negatively interprets the situation in the presence of more plausible alternative explanations. If persuaded to reflect on these more positive explanations, he may admit that he was biased in assessing the situation. Thus, the patient can be brought to the realization that he is perverting the facts, fitting them into pre-formed negative conclusions.

The third component of the triad is associated with a negative attitude towards one's own future. Looking to the future, the depressive sees there only an endless series of hardships and sufferings. He believes that he is destined to endure difficulties, disappointments, and hardships until the end of his days. Thinking about the things that he needs to do in the near future, he expects failure.

All other symptoms included in the depressive syndrome are considered in the cognitive model as the consequences of the activation of the above negative patterns. So, if a patient mistakenly believes that he is rejected by people, his emotional reaction will be as negative (sadness, anger) as in the case of real rejection. If he mistakenly considers himself an outcast, he will experience a feeling of loneliness.

Violations of motivation (for example, lack of will, lack of desires) can be explained by the distortion of cognitive processes. Pessimism and a sense of hopelessness paralyze the will. If a person is always disposed to defeat if he always expects a negative result, why should he set any goals or take on some business? In its extreme expression, the avoidance of problems and situations that seem unsolvable and unbearable takes the form of suicidal desires.

A depressed patient often sees a burden on others and, on the basis of this, concludes that everyone, including himself, will be better off if he dies. The increased dependence observed in depressed patients can also be explained in cognitive terms. Being convinced of his mediocrity and helplessness and seeing in everything only difficulties and barriers, the patient believes that he cannot cope even with the most banal task. He seeks help and support from others, who seem to him much more competent and capable than himself.

Finally, the cognitive model also explains the physical symptoms of depression. Apathy and loss of strength may be the result of the patient's conviction of the futility of his undertakings. A pessimistic view of the future (a sense of futility) can cause "psychomotor retardation."

The Structure of Depressive Thinking

Another important component of the cognitive model is the concept of circuitry. It helps explain why a depressed patient clings to his negative, painful, destructive ideas despite the obvious presence of positive factors in his life. Any situation consists of a great variety of incentives. The individual selectively responds to individual stimuli and, combining them into a pattern, conceptually conditions the situation. While different people may interpret the same situation differently, an individual person is usually consistent in their reactions to events of the same type. The comparative stability of cognitive patterns, which we call "patterns," is the reason that a person interprets situations of the same type in the same way. When a person is faced with an event, the scheme associated with this event is activated. A diagram is a kind of form for casting information into a cognitive formation (verbal or figurative representation). In accordance with the activated scheme, the individual eliminates, differentiates, and encodes information. He categorizes and evaluates what is happening, guided by his matrix of schemes.

The subjective structure of various events and situations depends on what patterns the individual uses. The scheme may remain in a deactivated state for a long time, but it is easily set in motion by a specific environmental stimulus (for example, a stressful situation). The individual's response to a specific situation is determined by the activated circuit. In psychopathological conditions such as depression, the perception of stimuli is impaired; he distorts the facts or perceives only those that fit into the dysfunctional schemes that dominate his mind. The normal process of correlating a pattern with a stimulus is disrupted by the invasion of these extremely active idiosyncratic patterns. As idiosyncratic schemes gain activity, the range of stimuli actualizing them expands; they can now be set in motion even by absolutely irrelevant stimuli. The patient almost loses control over his thought processes and is not able to use more adequate schemes.

In mild forms of depression, the patient, as a rule, is able to more or less objectively evaluate his negative thoughts. With the aggravation of depression, negative ideas become more and more powerful, despite the absence of any objective evidence of their legitimacy. Since dominant idiosyncratic patterns lead to distortion of reality and systematic errors in thinking, a depressed patient is less and less inclined to recognize the fallacy of his interpretations. In the most severe cases, the idiosyncratic pattern reigns supreme in the patient's thinking. The patient is completely captured by preservative, repetitive negative thoughts; it is extremely difficult for him to concentrate on external stimuli (for example, reading or questions of the interlocutor), and he is incapable of voluntary mental activity (computing, solving problems, memories). In this case, we conclude that the idiosyncratic cognitive structure has become autonomous. The depressive cognitive formation can be so independent of external stimulation that the individual becomes completely insensitive to changes that occur in his immediate environment.

Incorrect Processing of Information

The patient's conviction in the reliability of his negative ideas is maintained thanks to the following systematic errors in thinking (see Beck, 1967).

- Arbitrary inferences: the patient draws conclusions and conclusions in the absence of facts supporting these conclusions, or contrary to the presence of opposing facts.

- Selective abstraction: the patient draws his conclusions based on anyone fragment of the situation taken out of context, ignoring its more significant aspects.

- ▪ Generalization: the patient draws a general rule or draws global conclusions based on one or more isolated incidents and then evaluates all other situations, relevant and irrelevant, based on pre-formed conclusions.

- Overestimation and underestimation: mistakes made in assessing the significance or importance of an event are so great that they lead to a distortion of facts.

- Personalization: the patient is inclined to correlate external events with his own person, even if there is no reason for such a correlation.

- Absolutism, dichotomic of thinking: the patient is inclined to think in extremes, to divide events, people, actions, etc. into two opposite categories, for example, "perfect — flawed," "good — bad," "holy — sinful." Speaking about himself, the patient usually chooses a negative category.

In order to better understand depressive thinking disorders, it is useful to consider them in terms of the individual's ways of structuring reality. If we divide the latter into "primitive" and "mature," it is obvious that in depression, a person structures experience in comparatively primitive ways. His judgments about unpleasant events are global. The meanings and meanings presented in the stream of his consciousness are extremely negative in color; they are categorical and evaluative in content, which gives rise to an extremely negative emotional reaction. In contrast to this primitive type of thinking, mature thinking easily integrates life situations into a multidimensional structure (and not into just one category) and evaluates them in quantitative rather than qualitative terms, correlating them with each other and not with absolute standards. Primitive thinking reduces the complexity, diversity, and variability of human experience, reducing it to a few of the most general categories.

It seems to us that these typical characteristics of depressive thinking are similar to the features of children's thinking described by Piaget (1932/1960). Conventionally, we call this type of thinking "primitive" in order to separate it from the more adaptive thinking observed in the late stages of development. A depressed patient, as noted above, is inclined to see what is happening to him only deprivation and defeat (one-dimensional thinking) and is inclined to believe that they will never end. He considers himself to be "losers" (categorical, evaluative judgment) and believes that he is doomed to eternal suffering.

Predisposition to Depression

The cognitive model offers a hypothesis of a predisposition to depression. According to our theory, negative ideas about one's own person, one's future, and the surrounding world are formed in a person on the basis of early experience. These ideas (schemes) can, for the time being, be in a latent state - they are activated by specific circumstances similar to those that are responsible for introducing a negative attitude.

For example, a divorce can activate the concept of irreversible loss in a person who survived the death of a father or mother in childhood. In the same way, physical injury or illness can cause depression, activating a person's latent belief that they are doomed to torment and suffering. However, unpleasant events do not necessarily have a depressive effect; the latter is observed only if a person, by virtue of his cognitive organization, is especially sensitive to this type of situation.

If the average individual, even in extremely traumatic situations, does not lose interest in life and the ability to assess its other positive aspects adequately, then the thinking of a person predisposed to depression is significantly narrowed, which leads to the formation of a persistent negative attitude to all aspects of life.

The cognitive model of depression has received a lot of empirical evidence. The data of naturalistic and clinical observations, the results of experimental studies (Beck, Rush, 1978) confirm our concept of a "cognitive triad." Some studies have found cognitive deficits (e.g., diminished abstract thinking ability, increased attention selectivity) in depressed and suicidal patients.

Reciprocal Interaction Model

Our cognitive theory of depression may seem one-sided to someone, because so far, we have been talking mainly about the "intrapsychic" aspects of depression, leaving aside the patient's interpersonal experience. In part, this one-sidedness is intentional; we consciously sought to concentrate the reader's attention on the methods of constructing reality used by the depressed patient. However, it's time to talk about what role a patient's relationship with people around him (family, friends, colleagues, employers, etc.) plays in depression.

As Bandura (1977) emphasizes, each person influences other people through their behavior. Falling into a depression, a person moves away from those around him that are significant to him. These "significant others," feeling rejected, can begin to criticize a person, which, in turn, activates or exacerbates his tendency to self-abase (or rejection by others is the first link in the chain of events leading to depression). Negative ideas and ideas actualized as a result of this lead the patient (who at that time may have all the signs of clinical depression) to more and more isolation. This vicious circle can exist for quite some time, as a result of which the patient becomes unable to adequately perceive people's attempts to demonstrate his love and affection to him.

On the other hand, harmonious interpersonal relationships serve as a kind of buffer that protects a person from deep depression. A strong system of social support, providing the patient with visible evidence that he is loved by people and dear to them, neutralizes his tendency to self-abasement. In addition, family members and friends of a depressed patient can help cure him by acting as representatives of social reality and helping the patient verify the validity of his negative thoughts and ideas. If the patient's relationship with significant others is seriously violated and is one of the factors exacerbating depression, then this or that form of conjugal or family therapy may be prescribed.

However, it should be emphasized that not all depressed patients are equally susceptible to the effects of significant others. In some cases, even the most favorable environmental influences are powerless before the inexorable course of depression.

"Traps" of Cognitive Therapy

As our observations show, specialists in cognitive therapy make the following very common mistakes.

Neglect of the therapeutic relationship.

A beginner may be so fascinated by cognitive therapy techniques that he completely overlooks the importance of establishing a strong therapeutic relationship with the patient. Interpersonal problems are perhaps the most common among those faced by therapists, starting to practice a cognitive approach. The therapist has no right to forget that he is not alone, but together with another person, he is busy solving an extremely difficult task. Here are some guidelines to help the therapist establish a good relationship with the patient.

1. The patient should be able to express and discuss their emotions (chapter 2).

2. It is important to consider what style of communication the patient is used to. The therapist must be able to adapt his style, "adapting" to a particular patient. Fortunately, cognitive therapy allows the therapist to form a wide repertoire of styles. The therapist can be very active with one patient and be more restrained with the other. Some patients require ongoing leadership, while others themselves are ready to take the initiative and need only encouragement.

3. The therapist must understand that due to depression, the patient has a disrupted ability to normal interpersonal communication

and interaction, that it is extremely difficult for him to concentrate, formulate and state his problems, establish emotional contact with the interlocutor. Some depressed patients literally go numb; in this case, the therapist has to make assumptions about what worries the patient and carefully monitor his reaction in order to confirm or refute his guesses.

4. It should be borne in mind that depressed patients are extremely sensitive to statements and actions that can be interpreted as evidence of rejection, indifference, or disapproval. The reactions and interpretations of the patient, of course, provide the key to understanding his problems, but the therapist must always be alerted to catch and constructively use these erroneous interpretations.

Traditionalism, Inconsistency, and Excessive Caution

Novice therapists often fall into one of two extremes. Some, eager to quickly master the technical side of the matter, stand in the position of a Specialist and how parrots repeat what they saw and heard at the seminars, instead of integrating the new knowledge organically. These therapists are like robots; they speak in clichés and use, as it seems to them, "ingenious" techniques, which, however, are easily guessed by a patient who is familiar with materials on cognitive therapy. Others, taking advantage of the fact that the cognitive model allows for flexible use, try to "test" all your favorite techniques and techniques, without wondering how they are suitable for this patient at the moment. They grab hold of one technique, then another, without bothering to evaluate their effectiveness.

On the other hand, many neophytes are overly cautious, afraid to do something "wrong," and thereby upset the patient. Therefore, they are either silent or mechanically to follow all the requirements governing the treatment procedure. Fortunately, the general strategy of cognitive therapy provides a number of "safety" points, such as feedback from the patient, helping the therapist to make sure that the patient understands him correctly and smooth out the unproductive reactions that the patient may have in response to those or other techniques, suggestions or behaviors of a therapist (chapters 3 and 4).

Reductionism and an Overly Simplistic Approach

Beginners tend to see in cognitive therapy only a way to make a person realize and correct their negative thoughts, forgetting that this method is based on a cognitive theory of emotional disorders. We repeat that it is extremely difficult if at all possible, to engage in cognitive therapy without understanding its theoretical principles successfully.

Although the cognitive model attempts to explain very complex disorders using a limited number of concepts, it must be remembered that each patient presents a specific pattern of psychopathology. There is no universal pattern for collecting data and changing idiosyncratic patterns that is equally applicable to all patients. Considering that in our therapeutic guide, we translate the techniques and principles of cognitive therapy into the language of specific operations, we consider it necessary to warn beginners against attempts to conduct therapy, "according to the cookbook." Cognitive therapy is a holistic approach, although it implies a certain sequence of clearly defined, discrete steps. Therefore, it is important for the therapist to find a "middle ground" between excessive concreteness and excessive abstraction, atomism, and globalism.

Didacticism and a Tendency for Excessive Interpretations

Questions are one of the important components of cognitive therapy. It is not enough to simply indicate to the patient the distortion of his perception, that there is a negative thought between the event and his emotional reaction - such an intervention usually turns out to be ineffective. The therapist should use an inductive approach and ask questions that reveal the one-sided logic of the patient.

Another advantage of the inductive procedure is that the patient learns to ask himself questions. It is as if he "hears" the therapist's voice asking him: "What facts is this conclusion based on?", "What will be the most adaptive action now?" Learning to recognize and test his assumptions, the patient develops healthy empiricism that serves as a barrier to the formation of unrealistic inferences.

Paradoxically, the tendency found in some therapists to read the instructions and present their own conclusions to the patient regarding his thoughts has sometimes a positive effect. The thing is that due to the "suggestive" nature of this approach, the patient "produces" facts that support the therapist's conclusions.

Nevertheless, visible improvements in the patient's condition, as a rule, are short-term in nature, and after some time, a relapse of the disease is observed.

Of course, it is very important to educate the patient, to explain to him how depression occurs and how it can be defeated by means of cognitive therapy. However, the therapist must ensure that the patient does not recklessly accept his explanations on faith, but critically comprehends and checks them on his own experience.

The "Superficial" Approach

Neophytes sometimes overlook the importance of revealing hidden meanings. Correction of the patient's automatic thoughts is essential, but not the most important element of cognitive therapy. Of fundamental importance is the discovery of the totality of meanings given by the patient to various events. Often the patient cannot accurately formulate what this or that situation means to him, and the therapist has to "get to the bottom" of these hidden meanings.

Let us explain what was said by the following example. The patient sent his manuscript to the publishing house and was refused, which automatically gives rise to the thought: "This is a failure. All my efforts went down the drain. I will never write anything worthwhile." However, if the therapist asks the patient, "What does this refusal mean to you as a person? How does it affect your future? What kind of experiences does he give you?" He may receive the following answer: "This means that I am not capable of anything. I will never succeed. You can put an end to my career ... I will never be happy. "

Working only with the material at hand, discussing only the patient's thoughts, the therapist misses an extremely important point - the hidden subjective meaning of the event. The therapist must help the patient formulate not only the expected consequences of the event but also examine the premises that determine the subjective value and anticipated consequences of what happened. So, in this case, the patient proceeds from assumptions such as: "The only failure prophesies a chain of failures" and "I will never be happy if my work remains unpublished."

For the same reasons, the therapist cannot be content with superficial explanations; he needs to check the accuracy of the introspection of the patient. It is impossible to be sure that you understand the whole gamut of human experiences without penetrating into his "phenomenal world." The feedback system provided for cognitive therapy allows the therapist to verify the correctness of his perception of the patient's inner world.

Continuous Self-Examination

The patient should be encouraged to investigate the subjective meanings of events during the course of therapy, and especially at its end. The therapist, together with the patient, should even consider such an event as the prospect of completing a therapeutic course.

The Dependence of Learning on the Condition of the Patient and the Assistance of Loved Ones

We found that patients are easier to learn to analyze and overcome precisely "burning," burning problems and difficulties. If depressive feelings and negative thoughts associated with them are noted in the patient directly during the therapy session, it is easier for the therapist to teach the patient how to work with them. Therefore, it is reasonable to schedule a meeting between the therapist and the patient at a time when the likelihood of a problem situation is high. For example, a feeling of loneliness is exacerbated in many patients in the evenings and on weekends. Sometimes a telephone conversation helps to solve an unexpected problem. Instead of trying to squeeze the treatment process into the "Procrustean bed" of random appointments, the therapist or his assistant can visit the patient at home to help deal with problems that arise in this particular situation (for example, housework or homework). We found that such visits are often more fruitful than appointments in the doctor's office. In this regard, our data confirm the modern concept of training, which states: skills acquired by a person in a particular state will be actualized by him more likely in this state than in others. So, to teach the patient to overcome suicidal impulses is best when he is close to suicide.

Since home visits are not always possible or convenient for one reason or another, you can involve someone from the patient's family members or friends. Having learned the use of specific therapeutic strategies, such a person can act as the "governor" of the therapist.

Chapter 2

The Role of Emotions in Cognitive Therapy

It is well known that the richness of human experience is determined by the diversity of feelings and emotions. For most people, it is feelings or emotions that are the most certain, most real source of information about the world. Without a free play of emotions, we would never know the joy of discovery, would not experience excitement at the sight of a loved one, and funny would not amuse us. Deprived of the shades of feelings that make us worry, we would lead a mechanical existence as purely "cerebral" beings. In a sense, a depressed person is like a "cerebral" being. He understands the meaning of the joke, but the joke does not make him fun. He describes the attractive qualities of a wife or child while not experiencing either satisfaction or pride. He eats his favorite dish, listens to his favorite music, and does not get any pleasure from it. The paradox is that the dulling of positive feelings is adjacent to the extreme tension of negative emotions; it seems that the whole supply of feelings gushed through the open gateways of sadness, apathy, and longing.

Therefore, when working with a depressed patient, we must constantly remember the severity of his loss - the inability to experience pleasure, joy, fun, affection - and the intensity of the anguish that engulfed him. Quite often, it is precisely the lack of former love for loved ones and the loss of interest in life that compels a person to consult a doctor. Further investigation, of course, reveals other signs of depression. The terms "cognitive therapy" and "rational therapy" often mislead the uninitiated, giving rise to the idea of a set of intellectualized rituals that ignore human feelings and sensations and reduce the entire wealth of human relationships to sterile dialectics. A rational or cognitive approach is often confused with the philosophical school of rationalism and the rationalist movement, pioneered by Ayn Rand and Nathaniel Brandon. In this regard, Albert Ellis, wanting to emphasize the importance of emotions, renamed his "rational psychotherapy" into "rational-emotive therapy."

The goal of cognitive therapy - weakening emotional distress and other symptoms of depression - is achieved through the study and correction of erroneous interpretations, dysfunctional attitudes, and maladaptive behavior of the patient. When working with cognitive formations, the therapist must carefully monitor changes in the patient's mood. He cannot limit himself to identifying pathological cognitive structures and tracing the connections between negative thoughts and negative emotions of the patient; he must understand the patient's painful feelings and empathize with them. The same care should be taken to the slightest signs of pleasure or fun on the part of the patient, encouraging these pleasant emotions, if possible.

In our culture, not affected by the influence of Stoic philosophy, a sense of pleasure and positive emotions are highly valued. A person who has lost the ability to experience pleasant feelings feels "not quite human." Therefore, the patient's messages about the feelings he is experiencing carry information about how the treatment is progressing and can serve as a guide when applying specific therapeutic strategies.

It must be emphasized, however, that cognitive therapy does not attach exceptional importance to the study and promotion of the patient's emotional experience, as is customary in experimental therapy schools where subject experience is crucial. A common drawback of these "reactive" approaches is that they do not see the connection between irrational and dysfunctional ideative formations, on the one hand, and inadequate emotional reactions, on the other, and deny the possibility of mitigating these reactions by rational means.

Meanwhile, many authors, wondering about the mechanisms of the therapeutic effect achieved as a result of the use of various types of psychotherapy, quite reasonably declare that their effectiveness is largely determined by cognitive modification. For example, compelling clinical and empirical data have been obtained that indicate that improvements in the patient's state in the course of systematic desensitization are mediated by cognitive restructuring. As Ellis points out, cognitive reorganization is the main driving force behind the success of "sensory" therapeutic approaches, such as Gendlin's experience therapy.

It can already be considered proof that the so-called "emotional problems" are associated not only with the initiation of a certain emotion, but have a much more complex background. Serious empirical studies have shown the crucial role of cognitive factors in the onset and mitigation of anxiety (Lazarus, 1966; Meichenbaum, 1977) and anger (Novaco, 1975). Therefore, in order to avoid misunderstandings, it would be more correct to speak not about "emotional disorders," but about "psychological disorders."

Cognitive therapy is not limited to the theoretical study of the relationship of emotions with cognitive processes, but also actively uses various "emotional techniques." We found that the spontaneous expression and intensification of emotions caused by the techniques of "sensory awareness" and "floods" are an important aid in treating the patient - if they are woven into the general outline of a cognitive modification program. In fact, if an essential part of cognitive therapy for depression is the relationship between an unpleasant emotion and its cognitive structure or prevailing attitude, there is no need to explain how important it is to identify the patient's emotional reactions correctly.

Identification and Expression of Emotions

In view of the important role assigned to emotions in the cognitive model of personality and psychopathology, and in order to avoid a mechanistic approach to therapy, the therapist must constantly monitor and evaluate the patient's emotions, as well as monitor his own emotional reactions. Timely identified inadequate or overly violent reactions can signal cognitive impairment.

Some patients (especially men) tend to deny their feeling of sadness initially, but after all other depressive symptoms have cleared up, they tend to recognize and acknowledge the emotions they experience. It is significant that many of those who choose the statement "I don't feel sadness" from the first set of alternatives to the "Depression Scale" Beck, after filling out the entire questionnaire, change their answer to "I feel sad."

The patient may talk about a wide variety of symptoms associated with depression (for example, loss of energy, sleep disturbances, loss of appetite, negative attitudes), but does not admit to himself that he is sad or sad - instead, he complains of loss or weakening positive feelings, speaks of the lack of previous attachment and love for a spouse, children, friends, about the loss of interest in life, about the impossibility to enjoy the activities that once pleased him. In other words, he is aware of his apathy, but not sadness.

When determining the patient's emotional reactions, one must remember the semantic trap that many therapists fall into who take any phrase preceded by the words "I feel" for verbalization of emotion. People tend to express their thoughts, opinions, assumptions with the words "I feel," or "I feel." When a person says: "I feel insignificant" or: "I feel that I will not be happy if I do not succeed," he verbalizes a certain idea, possibly associated with feeling. Or he simply "cautious," and hides behind his statement: "I understand that I'm probably wrong, and therefore I'd better say, "I feel" than, "I think."

Experience-oriented therapists sometimes grab onto the prologue of the statement ("I feel") and then repeat "So you feel ...", mistakenly believing that this path leads them to the "true" feelings of the patient. A cognitive therapist should immediately translate "I feel ..." to "you believe ..."

After the patient has understood the difference between feeling (sadness, joy, anger, anxiety) and thought, you can try to assess how well he manages to recognize and name his own feelings. In general, depressed patients identify their feelings fairly easily and correctly associate the occurrence or intensification of unpleasant emotions with specific situations. At times, however, one gets the impression that the patient separates feelings from the rest of the behavior. One patient, for example, every time after an unpleasant event, felt a lump in her throat. Based on this, she concluded that she was experiencing sadness, and only after that, she really felt sadness. Another patient began to cry before realizing her unpleasant feelings. She said: "I am crying, which means I am sad." Upon further investigation, she discovered that she felt longing even before she wanted to cry.

The inclusion in the patient's sphere of consciousness of the unpleasant emotions experienced by him also helps with a thorough history. For example, a 35-year-old housewife complained that during the year, she noted increased fatigue, weakness, and apathy, although, at the reception, she looked quite cheerful and claimed that she did not feel unhappy and did not feel longing. She literally told the psychiatrist the following: "I don't understand why I constantly feel so tired. I have a wonderful husband and wonderful children. I am completely satisfied with my marriage; in fact, I have everything that a person can wish for." Fulfilling the therapist's request to tell in more detail about the relationship with her husband, she began to describe a specific case from her family life and suddenly burst into tears - to her own amazement and surprise of the therapist. It was difficult for her to reconcile her sense of sadness with the rainbow-colored ideas cherished by her about her marriage.

Talking about some of the most typical acts of her husband, she sobbed. Then, having calmed down a bit, she said: "You know ... I probably didn't fully realize how much it hurts me." She stated that now she feels an unprecedented longing. Longing intensified as the patient increasingly understood that her relationship with her husband was far from ideal, and was a kind of barometer showing the depth of family problems. After the patient learned to recognize her negative feelings, she was able to attach them to her knowledge, namely, "He is inattentive to others," "He always does what is convenient for him," "He does not care what I want," "He treats me like an unconscious child."

As a result of a short therapeutic consultation, the patient found that the refusal to use absolute measures when evaluating her husband leads to a weakening of her melancholy and amelioration of other depressive symptoms. Before therapy, it was common for her to evaluate her husband from an "all or nothing" position, to see in him either only good or only bad traits and "bad grades" were immediately discarded (and forgotten). Following the advice of the therapist, she began to declare her husband about her own desires more clearly and was surprised to find that he was sympathetic to them. Almost at the same time, her former cheerfulness and energy returned to her. It is curious that for 15 years after that consultation, she did not have depressive symptoms.

Thus, the central problems of the patient were:

a) A tendency to think in extremes, and

b) A tendency to deny thoughts and feelings that were discordant with her romantic ideas about life.

Even before marriage, she convinced herself that her chosen one was perfection itself, and idealized her relationship with him. In fact, her husband, despite all his charm and attractiveness, turned out to be an egocentric, imperious person, and she, cherishing her dream of harmonious family life, completely obeyed his desires. But from time to time, she found herself thinking about her husband very badly (for example: "He is an insensitive, cruel man"), and then anguish, anger, and irritation rolled over her. She drove away bad thoughts from herself, but unpleasant feelings remained with her. She tried to suppress dysphonic experiences because they were contrary to her self-image as "the one who was lucky." Her apathy and fatigue were largely due to a desperate desire to deny troubles. In addition, expecting too much from her husband and receiving too little, she experienced chronic disappointment, which, like acid, corroded her vitality and spontaneity.

Having learned to meet and be aware of her emotions fearlessly, the patient was able to perceive her husband more realistically, ceased to see in him only a Knight in shining armor or only a Blue Beard. The final stage of therapy was to be the restructuring of the relationship of the spouses, which was achieved through role-playing games in the framework of assertiveness training.

This case proves how skillfully conducted a patient survey is of great importance. Before embarking on a study of dysfunctional thoughts and erroneous conclusions, the therapist must clarify how the patient feels and experiences. In addition, the case perfectly illustrates the importance of a detailed study of the patient's current life; the therapist cannot take on faith global statements like: "I am doing well" or vice versa: "I am doing badly." In contrast to this lady, most depressed patients are prone to negative generalizations, which tend to crumble upon careful examination of the details.

And the last thing I would like to say in connection with the question of the importance of encouraging the patient to express feelings. We found that the sympathy and empathy of the therapist become a real discovery for some patients. So, one of the patients, a policeman by profession, burst into tears, feeling that his despair was warmly received by the therapist. He cried for five minutes and then admitted: "The last time I cried was when I was a child." From that moment on, he felt relieved and began to crawl out of his lingering depression.

The Role of Emotions in a Therapeutic Relationship

Obviously, almost all components of a therapeutic relationship have an emotional aspect. In the normal development of a therapeutic relationship, the patient, as a rule, has warm feelings for his therapist, believes in the success of treatment, feels gratitude to the therapist, feels safe at the thought of an upcoming meeting with the therapist, and looks forward to it. The therapist's reactions to the patient also have an emotional connotation: he empathizes with the patient, takes care of him, wants to help, and rejoices if he succeeds.

The effectiveness of a therapeutic relationship is largely dependent on the patient's ability to experience and express emotions during a therapeutic session. Depressed patients often have a sense of their own "unnaturalness." It is difficult for them to tell others about their negative feelings; they are ashamed and forced to hide them behind the social facade. This fact is interpreted by them as dishonesty towards people. Therefore, many of them say that the very possibility of open expression of emotions, the ability to "be yourself," helps them to feel honest and sincere.

The range of emotionalized attitudes that cause shame in patients is very wide. This is a weakening of the ability to show or even experience love, chronic irritation in relation to loved ones, constant anxiety. In addition, many patients are ashamed of their bad mood, realizing that it does not correspond to their completely prosperous life situation. From many of them, one has to hear: "I have everything that you can wish for, but it does not make me happy and does not bring me happiness." The patient scolds himself for not feeling grateful to fate, feels guilty in front of people, and unworthy of their kindness. Moreover, in some patients, a marked deterioration is noted when relatives and friends begin to show them special attention or care.

Only in the context of therapy does the patient have the opportunity to discuss their emotional reactions freely. But even here, the patient is not inclined to talk about his "shameful" reactions until the therapist establishes a rapport with him and touches on this painful topic. "Self-disclosure" relieves stress caused by suppression or withholding of the senses. Seeing that the therapist accepts and understands his negative reactions, the patient is freed from guilt and constant self-flagellation. Many patients are relieved if they manage to cry during the session. Free crying, apparently, initially has a therapeutic effect, and this effect is realized if the patient feels that he can openly express his emotions, and no one will condemn him for them. However, some patients (especially men) consider crying a manifestation of weakness. Others are not at all able to control their crying and can cry the whole session; in this case, the therapist has to use special strategies (distraction or behavioral control) to alleviate this problem. As will be shown in one of the following chapters, learning how to control crying can be an important prerequisite for constructive communication between the therapist and the patient.

The therapist must constantly remember that he is not treating himself but the patient. In other words, he should not use therapy to solve his own problems. We have heard of individual therapists who empathize with their patients so much that they cry with them. The therapeutic value of such an interchange is that it serves as a bridge connecting the therapist with the patient. However, it must be remembered that only very experienced therapists decide on this, knowing exactly at what point it is appropriate to give free rein to their own feelings.

Release of Emotions

Speaking of "releasing emotions," we, of course, use a metaphor. The metaphor is based on the idea of a certain internal and cumulative source of emotion. The internal logic of this view suggests the need for a periodic discharge of "accumulated energy." However, many therapists take this verbal turn too literally and urge the patient to release emotion without burdening himself with the question of whether he really is experiencing it. Some representatives of the school of "experiences" believe that "accumulated emotions" are the source of all problems and that it is only necessary to "release" feelings, how a miracle will happen, and the patient will be cured. Of course, the patient, expressing his feelings, may feel improvement, but this therapeutic effect, as a rule, is fragile; moreover, if therapy is reduced only to experiencing and expressing emotions, the patient's condition may subsequently worsen.

Unlike therapists, patients sometimes go to the other extreme. Some are simply ashamed to express their feelings. They are ready to talk about their negative emotions, but consider such forms of expression of feelings as sobbing, angry outbursts, screaming or clenching their fists as shameful, and thereby close the possibility of "catharsis" for themselves. In such cases, you should first find out what exactly prevents the patient from expressing their feelings openly, then to jointly eliminate these internal prohibitions.

It is necessary to make it clear to the patient that there are no shameful or "unacceptable" feelings, that any feeling can be the subject of discussion. However, the therapist must appropriately structure the session so that it does not appear that all of her time has been devoted to "emotion." If the patient's emotional reactions are based on irrational ideas or seem excessive, it is important to encourage him to explore the cognitive premises of these feelings. Quite often, patients direct their irritation to the therapist. The therapist must be prepared for such a situation and must remember that these negative reactions are part of the normal spectrum of emotions in people suffering from psychological disorders, and therefore they must be treated calmly. However, the patient's constant attacks on the therapist can reduce the productivity of therapeutic sessions.

In the same way, warm feelings also sometimes pose a problem. Some patients get stuck in their gratitude to the therapist and are no longer able to move on. The notorious "transfer" reaction may also have a counterproductive effect. Some patients try to stop the therapy, suffering from unrequited love for the therapist, while others, on the contrary, are constantly looking for a meeting with him in order to make love to him or in the hope of fulfilling their erotic dreams. If the patient tries to stop treatment, the therapist should encourage him to talk about his feelings in order to explore them together. In any case, there are a number of techniques to help overcome this kind of reaction.

For example, if a patient "falls in love" with her therapist, he may suggest that she write down what attracts her to him, and then discuss how her current image corresponds to reality. In such a study, it is usually found that the patient idealizes the therapist, attributing to him non-existent virtues.

The work with the patient's angry reactions is similarly structured. The therapist asks the patient to write what exactly annoys him in the therapist, and then together, they examine the list of negative characteristics to confirm them with specific examples. These techniques are woven into the general process of "reality testing," which is an integral part of cognitive therapy.

It is very important to correctly determine at what moment the patient's angry tirade should be interrupted, because, on the one hand, the patient should be able to express his negative feelings, and on the other hand, he should not be allowed to reach the boiling point, when the anger becomes uncontrollable and becomes self-generating quality. After expressing anger, it's not difficult for some patients to calmly sit back in a chair and analyze your reaction; in other words, they spontaneously begin to check whether there were real grounds for this reaction. Other patients require constant monitoring by a therapist to achieve a therapeutic balance between emotional expression and rational discussion. The results of some experimental work by Robert Green and Edward Murray (Green, Murray, 1975) show that emotional release facilitates the process of rational restructuring.

If the patient begins to feel better after expressing emotions, this may be the beginning of a favorable cycle. Many depressed patients no longer hope for improvement, and this positive experience, like any signs of improvement, helps them gain hope and strengthens their motivation to work with the therapist.

Chapter 3

Therapeutic Relationships
in the Context of Cognitive Therapy

Cognitive therapy consists of a number of specific techniques, the use of which is systematic and consistent in nature and is carried out, taking into account the individual characteristics of the patient. Like other psychotherapeutic techniques, cognitive techniques involve a certain type of interpersonal relationship. The way the therapist uses the methods and techniques of cognitive therapy directly affects the nature of the relationship between the therapist and the patient, and vice versa.

This chapter describes the general characteristics of therapeutic cooperation and the quality of the therapist, which, in our opinion, facilitate the use of specific cognitive therapy techniques. Guided by these principles, the therapist can evaluate their attitudes and level of technical skill. In addition, this chapter discusses how to prepare a patient for therapy, how to plan treatment, and how to conduct targeted therapy sessions.

Requirements for the Therapist

General requirements that a therapist must meet in order to successfully implement cognitive therapy (like other types of psychotherapy) include a warm attitude to the patient, the ability to empathy and sincerity. Immediately make a reservation that these qualities and attitudes, if they are overly accentuated, can undermine therapeutic cooperation. On the other hand, the skillful use of these qualities significantly increases the effectiveness of therapy.

We think that the above characteristics are necessary, but not the only condition for achieving the optimal therapeutic effect. However, the presence and proper use of these qualities help the therapist create an environment conducive to the effective use of specific cognitive techniques and techniques.

We believe it necessary to make one warning. Cognitive and behavioral techniques seem extremely simple, and this outward simplicity can mislead the neophyte. The newcomer to cognitive therapy is sometimes so enthralled by the technical side of things that he completely forgets about the human aspects of the therapeutic relationship. He communicates with the patient not as a person with a person, but as a computer with a computer. Thus, the approach of some young therapists, the most successful in applying various methods and techniques, seemed to patients mechanistic, manipulative, and not taking into account the interests of the patient. Therefore, the therapist must, firstly, get rid of the feeling of his own infallibility and, secondly, he must keep in mind that the techniques and methods described in this book involve tactful and humane use.

Warm Attitude Towards the Patient

A depressed patient, by virtue of his illness, is inclined to see a burden for the therapist and seek constant confirmation of his coldness and indifference. In order to overcome and correct this distorted image, which makes fruitful therapeutic cooperation impossible, the therapist must be sincerely interested in the patient and must constantly demonstrate his warm attitude towards him. It is important to remember that the decisive factor in the patient's reaction is his perception of the therapist rather than the actual manifestations of the therapist's attitude.

On the other hand, the therapist needs to exercise some caution when expressing his caring attitude towards the patient. If the therapist takes too much care of the patient (or, more importantly, if the patient thinks so), this can cause a backlash. The patient may think: "I do not deserve such a good attitude" or: "I am deceiving him. He does not even suspect how insignificant I am." The patient may also misinterpret the therapist's motives: "He is insincere" or: "How can he feel good feelings for such insignificance?" Sometimes patients interpret the therapist's warm attitude as love affection and, in turn, begin to be attracted to the therapist (see chapter 2).

In short, it is important to maintain a balance in expressing warm feelings for the patient. If the patient unequivocally regards the lack of care on the part of the therapist as rejection, then the therapist's too cordial involvement can cause both negative and distorted-positive interpretations. Therefore, the therapist must carefully monitor that his attitude towards the patient does not become counterproductive.

To prevent such a development of events, it is useful from time to time to ask the patient how he perceives the therapist. Patient's answers not only help the therapist to correct their behavior but also carry information about the "pain points" and cognitive distortions.

The warm, accepting attitude of the therapist can be evidenced by the way he behaves with the patient, how he formulates his statements, the intonation structure of his speech. Understanding the importance of these sometimes-elusive nuances comes to the therapist with experience. In addition, experienced therapists know and feel at what point and at what stage of therapy open demonstrations of participation and cordiality are most appropriate. If, at the beginning of treatment, the patient, as a rule, needs open manifestations of a warm, accepting position of the therapist, then later, having convinced himself of the therapist's feelings, he no longer needs to be constantly confirmed.

Accurate Empathy

Accurate empathy is the therapist's ability to penetrate the patient's inner world and see and feel like the way the patient sees and feels it. In fact, the therapist seems to "fit into the skin" of the patient. If he manages to experience the same feelings that the patient experiences, he will be able to understand how the patient structures certain events and how he reacts to them, in addition, the therapist can in one way or another inform the patient that he shares some of his troubles and suffering, which will help the patient to verify the therapist's sensitivity and thereby contribute to his further self-disclosure. In this regard, accurate empathy is a prerequisite for therapeutic cooperation (see Rogers, 1951).

There are other obvious reasons for empathy. If the therapist is able to delve into the patient's expectations and, to some extent, share them, it will be easier for him to explain the patient's unproductive behavior without resorting to value judgments. For example, he will be able to understand that the so-called "resistance" by which the patient responds to a request to fill out a questionnaire, or his "negative attitude" to homework is actually caused by his own sense of incompetence and hopelessness, - the patient simply does not believe in his ability to cope with these assignments. A sensitive therapist is able to understand that "cynicism" and anger, which are often observed in depressed patients, are a consequence of their grievances and disappointments.

Empathy helps the therapist to overcome the natural irritation that occurs in him in response to outwardly cynical or nihilistic statements and actions of the patient. Trying to penetrate the microcosm of the patient, the therapist is already less prone to antitherapeutic behavior. Moreover, only by "trying" on himself the negative attitudes and thoughts of the patient, the therapist can find an effective antidote or strong counterarguments for these negative ideas. As the therapist "comprehends" the patient's inner world, he must check the accuracy of his understanding, and for this, he needs to check his feelings with the feelings of the patient constantly.

The therapist must ensure that his own settings and expectations are not projected onto the patient; otherwise, he may distort the patient's messages. If, for example, a mother has died in a patient, this does not necessarily mean that he is saddened or upset by this fact. Some patients see death as a deliverance from a cruel, unjust world. The therapist, together with the patient, must track what significance he gives to such events.

On the other hand, the therapist cannot rely solely on empathy because it can make him believe in the veracity of the patient's negative ideas and interpretations. Being content with the data given by the patient, the therapist can ultimately be sure that the patient correctly reflects reality. Along with penetration into the patient's inner world, the therapist must constantly compare the patient's introspective observations with objective data to establish how logical the patient is in his conclusions and conclusions.

In this regard, it is important to distinguish between empathy and sympathy. Sympathy is simply empathy and empathy. An overly sympathetic reaction from the therapist may prevent him from identifying and eliminating the source of patient suffering. Empathy also includes both an emotional and an intellectual component, namely, an understanding of the cognitive background of feelings; it also implies the ability to distance oneself from these feelings in the name of maintaining an objective approach to the patient's problems. An empathizing therapist understands what ideas have evoked the patient's feelings, but he is not obliged to agree with these ideas if they seem erroneous, illogical, or destructive. However, it should be remembered that the patient does not doubt the reliability of his assumptions and expectations, and therefore the therapist should not ignore them, brush aside or persuade the patient to "refuse" them.

Sincerity

Sincerity is an important component of any psychotherapy. The therapist, whom we call sincere, is honest with both himself and the patient. However, honesty should not be confused with crude directness. Since depressed people tend to see confirmation of their own inferiority and deficiencies in everything, the therapist has to combine honesty with diplomacy. Any direct utterance can be interpreted by the patient as a criticism or manifestation of hostility and rejection. Moreover, the anti-therapeutic effect may have praise, even absolutely sincere.

It is not enough for the therapist to simply be sincere; he must be able to find the right expression for his feelings and opinions in order to be correctly understood by the patient. To do this, he needs to delve into the patient's distortion system and "outsmart" the patient's prejudices and attitudes. An inexperienced therapist makes a mistake when he begins to convince the patient that he will definitely recover. Full of a sense of hopelessness, the patient, after such a "promise," usually begins to consider the therapist insincere, insufficiently informed, or simply stupid. (A much more effective way is to demonstrate to the patient that the painful symptoms can be alleviated as a result of correcting his false beliefs and defeatist behavior.) The therapist also does the wrong thing in one way or another trying to assure the patient of his allegiance; such assurances usually arouse suspicion among patients ("Why does he care so much about me?") or provide food for guilt ("I do not deserve such attention").

Therapeutic Interaction

Now that we have discussed the therapeutically valuable qualities of the therapist, it is time to talk about the mechanisms for developing and strengthening the therapeutic relationship. These relationships imply equal participation of the therapist and patient and are based on trust, mutual understanding, and cooperation. Cognitive and behavioral therapy requires the same atmosphere of therapeutic cooperation as inherent in psychodynamic therapy.

Basic Trust

The significance of basic trust in therapeutic relationships is perfectly illustrated by the following quote from Chassell (Chassell, 1975).

"The hidden factor is the existence of the basic trust, basic pseudo-trust, and basic distrust in patients. Patients who sincerely trust the therapist usually show a positive transference that is conducive to therapy; they perceive the therapist as an object that will help them overcome their difficulties, and use it for their own purposes, with great tolerance for his shortcomings, provided that these shortcomings do not contradict the current image too much. Patients with basic pseudo-confidence can show many amazing reactions to the therapist: they emphasize their need for addiction, check the therapist's patience, put him on a pedestal - and at the same time constantly doubt the honesty of his intentions. Patients with baseline with disbelief will not advance one iota in the treatment until this problem is at least partially resolved; they feel the slightest contradictions in the position of the therapist, as they attribute to him many non-existent motives. Apparently, the hysterical characters belong to the pseudo-trust group; I believe obsessive personalities too."

When establishing a trusting relationship with a patient, the cognitive therapist must strike a balance between autonomy (allowing the patient to speak out, plan his own time, etc.) and the need for structure (therapist's directiveness, taking the initiative, etc.); between reliability and responsiveness (being punctual, answering phone calls, etc.) and the need for certain boundaries (not doing what the patient can do for himself); between the desire to be "just human" (that is, to behave naturally and in a friendly manner) and the need to be objective. As a rule, at the initial stages of treatment, the therapist behaves more actively and is more "involved" in the patient's problems than in the second half of the course, when he encourages the patient to take the initiative (for example, to plan the session and homework independently).

Rapport

If, in the case of limited disorders, such as private phobias, the presence of rapport is not very important, then in the treatment of depression, rapport plays a decisive role. Rapport usually describes harmonious relationships between people. In psychotherapy, rapport includes both emotional and intellectual components. In the presence of rapport, the patient perceives the therapist as a person, a) who is tuned to his feelings and thoughts, b) who understands him, sympathizes with him, and sympathizes with him, c) who accepts him with all his "shortcomings." At the optimal level of understanding, the therapist and patient feel safe and comfortable with each other. Neither one considers it necessary to defend, be careful, or withhold something from each other. The ability to accept the patient as he is does not imply blind approval or agreement with everything the patient says; "Acceptance" rather implies a lack of appreciation for the person. It allows the patient to drop all social masks, abandon pretense, and be sincere, natural.

For the therapist, having rapport means being able to express their concerns and concern for the patient openly. Knowing that he and the patient are tuned to the same wave, the therapist is not afraid that his spontaneous statements and reactions will be misinterpreted.

Free expression of feelings by the patient, of course, facilitates the process of establishing rapport and helps the therapist to feel empathy. It is much easier to empathize with a patient when he openly expresses his feelings than when the therapist has to "pry" him out of them.

A reasonable expression of warm feelings for the patient, of course, has a therapeutic effect. Moreover, sometimes, it is useful for the therapist to admit to his "negative" feelings, such as disappointment, resentment, irritation. However, when dealing with a depressed patient, the therapist must be careful. It must be understood that the patient may misinterpret the therapist's sincerity. Due to their tendency to distortion and exaggeration, depressed patients often perceive the positive feelings of the therapist as a manifestation of insincerity or see in them an appeal to love or sexual relations. In the same way, an overly frank account of a therapist about his own problems can aggravate the patient's pessimistic mood ("He is too weak to help me").

There is no ready-made recipe for establishing rapport with the patient. When working with one patient, one behavior style (for example, seriousness, detachment of the therapist) is effective, while the other response well to the opposite style (for example, in a friendly, warm, "advancing" manner of behavior of the therapist).

In cases where the therapist manages to establish a rapport, he feels that his comments and comments elicit a response from the patient. The patient is relaxed, open; he declares his consent or nods in response to the therapist; in a word, his whole appearance speaks of interest and participation.

Rapport is not only an indicator but also one of the factors of the therapist's cooperation with the patient. For example, it can be used to teach a patient adaptive behavioral response. With rapport, the therapist becomes a kind of example for the patient. A patient who has confidence in a therapist is interested in continuing treatment and performing specific therapeutic procedures (e.g., homework). Rapport stimulates the patient to express himself freely. Negative thoughts and feelings that can cause the patient to interrupt therapy are more likely to surface if the patient trusts the therapist.

What contributes to the establishment and maintenance of rapport in the behavior of the therapist? Therapists come to many things "naturally" without conscious effort. Some qualities and reactions require upbringing and conscious use. A good basis for building rapport is elementary politeness. You should not make the patient wait; you need to remember important facts from his life, and you need to welcome the patient warmly. During the meeting, the therapist must maintain visual contact with the patient, monitor the content of his story, understand and reflect his feelings, tactfully formulate his questions and comments.

An important role is played by the appearance, manners, and facial expressions of the therapist. The best thing is to maintain warm neutrality and professionalism. The therapist should feel when he should speak, and when it is better to be silent. Obviously, the manner of constantly interrupting the patient does not contribute to the establishment of rapport. But if the therapist is silent all the time, does not direct the patient's story, allowing him to jump from one to the other, the patient may experience anxiety that will weaken rapport. The therapist needs to monitor his voice so that it sounds soft and unobtrusive. The choice of words and definitions is also important (it is better to talk, for example, about "unproductive ideas" than about "neurotic," "painful," or "irrational" thinking).

The therapist's own way of thinking and attitudes also has a certain meaning. Some therapists experience frustration and anger when the patient is passive or, as they think, "resists" the treatment. It is clear that such an attitude generates negative feelings in the patient and undermines the rapport.

At the initial stage, the therapist needs to find out the patient's expectations regarding therapy and inform the patient about the upcoming therapeutic process. So, we recommend discussing with the patient the duration of treatment, the frequency and duration of sessions, the tasks of each stage, and the possibility of alternating "black" and "bright" days.

Reflection of the patient's feelings in the form of a resume, analogy, or metaphor helps to strengthen the rapport. For example, one patient, who felt quite satisfactory, experienced a relapse and, having come to the reception, told the therapist about her suicidal thoughts. The therapist reminded her how, at the last session, she said: "Although at times I feel like a mouse, I know that I have the heart of a lion." This phrase not only resurrected in the patient the feelings and attitudes necessary to continue the struggle but also showed her that the therapist believes in her.

Therapeutic Collaboration

Getting the Source Data

The therapy process begins with the therapist trying to encourage the patient to cooperate, that is, form a therapeutic alliance with the patient. Unlike "supportive" and "relational" types of therapy, where therapeutic relationships play the role of a tool to alleviate the patient's suffering, in cognitive therapy, they are seen as a way of combining the efforts of the therapist and patient to achieve specific goals. In this sense, the therapist and patient constitute a "team." The starting point for their cooperation is a common interest in the patient's thoughts, feelings, desires, and behavior.

Together they try to determine what and how the patient thinks, on what his thoughts are based, what benefits the patient benefits, and what he loses as a result of his thinking. The unique contribution of the patient lies in the fact that he provides the initial data for the study, namely, informs the therapist about his thoughts, feelings, and desires. The therapist's task is to guide the patient, telling him what data is needed and how it can be used for therapeutic purposes.

Each stage of therapy is used to develop and deepen cooperation. First, the patient, prompted and led by a therapist, learns to recognize and record his automatic negative interpretations. The therapist and patient then begin to analyze these data to identify specific patterns of automatic thinking. What kind of events usually cause negative thoughts in a patient? How confident is the patient that these thoughts accurately describe the real event? What logical mistakes does the patient make when drawing conclusions about himself, his future, and the world around him? Perhaps he gives too much importance to negative facts and ignores positive facts? What is the content of his thoughts and ideas, are there recurring themes (can it be that the patient constantly evaluates his competence or the reaction of other people to his actions)?

Confirmation of Introspective Data

The therapist teaches the patient to analyze and evaluate their own thoughts objectively. Thoughts (or cognitive formations) of the patient act as psychological events that can be a more or less true reflection of real events and situations. The therapist and the patient jointly determine to what extent the conclusions and conclusions of the patient correspond to the observations and conclusions of other, disinterested persons, that is, they carry out a reality check. The therapist asks questions in order to determine if the patient attaches idiosyncratic significance to certain events.

Often, these idiosyncratic depressive formations are stereotyped and contain recurring themes, such as "I am not capable of anything" or "My life has failed." Having identified these topics, the therapist tactfully brings the patient to their awareness. Together, they try to determine what basic premises the patient comes from (for example: "Until I achieve perfection in everything, I am a failure"). Thus, the patient learns to identify their basic settings and verify their validity.

The Study of Prejudice

Verification of the validity of preconceptions requires the joint efforts of the therapist and patient. The therapist asks the patient to recall specific facts confirming the validity of these prejudices, as well as facts that would refute them. The therapist may also ask the patient to try to evaluate other people based on his beliefs in order to understand how consistent the patient is in his principles. When discussing the patient's attitudes, insulting labels must not be put on them or brushed aside from certain prejudices as "obviously illogical" or "completely ridiculous." The therapist must act gently, tactfully, while maintaining objectivity and consistency of judgment.

Experiment Planning

One of the most effective methods to verify the validity of a particular prejudice is an experiment. How is the experiment designed? In a sense, the work of the therapist and patient is akin to a detective investigation. First of all, they specify which basic setting of the patient is to be checked. Suppose they found that the patient proceeds from the belief: "If I actively defend my rights, I will push people away from me." Focusing on this "general rule," the therapist puts forward a particular hypothesis, that is, predicts a certain specific situation, and then, together with the patient, develops an experiment to verify this prognosis.

In this case, a particular hypothesis can be formulated as follows: "If I tell my boss that I'm tired and want to take a day off, he will say that I'm a lazy person who is trying to evade work." Perhaps the therapist and patient will decide that this hypothesis is subject to verification in real conditions, that the patient should really talk with his boss. In this case, the patient is required to provide a report on the experiment, which should indicate what the boss specifically said and what thoughts came to the mind of the patient after what happened. Based on these data, the therapist and patient evaluate the results of the experiment, considering all possible interpretations of the event. The final step is to compare real results with patient expectations.

Home Tasks

Strengthening therapeutic cooperation, to a large extent, contributes to such a form of work as homework. Any homework is a kind of experiment because it gives the patient the opportunity to take a fresh look at his problem. The therapist must necessarily justify the feasibility of the task and explain the ways of its implementation; otherwise, the patient will not have an incentive to work independently.

Patients often perceive homework as a test of legal capacity, competence, or motivation, or believe that they are required to complete the task "perfectly." The therapist tries to overcome these unrealistic, anti-therapeutic settings, actively encouraging the patient to talk about thoughts and feelings that arise before and after completing the task. Some patients, having successfully completed a small task, devalue their success, believing that "everyone can do it." The therapist's task is to identify and correct these cognitive distortions. The therapist, for example, can directly tell the patient: "The meaning of the task is to simply try to do this work, and not to do it as well as you did it before."

Chapter 4

The Structure of
Therapeutic Interviews

Guidelines for the Therapist

Understanding the "Personal Paradigm" Of the Patient

When working with a patient, the therapist must keep several important principles in mind. No matter how ridiculous the therapist's negative ideas and beliefs may seem, he must understand that the patient is firmly convinced of their validity and credibility. The patient sincerely believes that he is an unhappy, useless, flawed, useless creature, and this conviction remains in him even in the presence of numerous and very eloquent evidence to the contrary. These beliefs and ideas are organized into a system similar to the one that Kuhn (1962) writes about as a scientific "paradigm." The patient perceives and interprets events, being guided by the conceptual scheme dominating in his consciousness. As is the case with scientific views, a personal paradigm can be modified when a person encounters a certain anomaly that cannot be explained within the framework of the existing paradigm or contradicts it.

However, a depressed patient, as a rule, does not perceive the significance of events that refute his gloomy ideas about life. Negative ideas of the patient come to light already at the very beginning of treatment. Starting to figure out what these ideas are based on, we usually discover two data sources. Firstly, the patient recalls many facts from his past, which, as it seems to him, justify his negative point of view on himself. Secondly, he can talk about several facts from his real life, also seeing in them a proof of his innocence. Cognitive therapy focuses on the present: the therapist encourages the patient to collect data on current events and record their interpretations of these events. Clearly, false interpretations of current events are easier to correct because the data source is at hand. However, when working with some patients, the impression is that they are simply unable to accept fresh information if it contradicts their prejudices.

The following example illustrates how a patient comes to treatment, firmly convinced of the legitimacy of his negative image of self. The depressed patient, the mother of five children, stubbornly considered herself inept and stupid. In support of her own stupidity, she cited the following facts: while still a college student, she was afraid to take the last exam, as a result of which she was left without a diploma; unlike her husband, a doctor, she did not have a professional career; two of her children recently had problems at school (and this, in her opinion, indicated that she was a "bad mother").

During the first therapeutic session, the therapist tried to dissuade the patient. He said that according to the results of psychological testing, her intelligence coefficient is 135 points, but she brought a number of objections, calling the test results unreliable.

After several sessions, the patient spontaneously told the therapist about several, previously not mentioned, aspects of her past and present life: at school, she studied only "excellently"; she had a certificate of graduation from model school; her husband always said that she was smarter and quicker than him; at one time she took aerobatic classes; she has performed in amateur performances; she was once fond of photography; several times during dinner parties, she heard flattering assessments from her husband's colleagues (they considered her a charming woman and an interesting conversationalist).

Thus, the patient's negative ideas about herself, for all their external groundlessness, differed in their internal sequence; they were consistent with all her concepts, observations, and memories. The therapist tried to delve into the patient's personal paradigm, wanting to understand what her obviously erroneous conceptualizations and ideas are based on. Having looked at the patient with her own eyes, convinced of the internal objectivity of her ideas, he could no longer consider them stupid or stupid. (A frontal attack on a patient's personal paradigm, grossly undermining his methods of structuring and interpreting reality, usually has an anti-therapeutic effect.)

There is no need to rush to refute the negative ideas of the patient with some objective data (for example, telling the patient his IQ) - the patient may simply not perceive or distort this data. And the therapist, in this case, will be in the role of the enemy, instead of collaborating with the patient and directing him in the right direction. Only when the patient feels that the therapist has carefully "studied his case" and understood his experiences, will he be ready to consider the opposite data presented to him and experimentally verify the reliability of his beliefs.

Avoid Value Judgments and Labeling

We recommend that the therapist treat the patient as a person who has problems or feeds irrational beliefs. When communicating with the patient, one should not resort to professional jargon and stick certain labels on the patient ("aggressive," "passive," "masochist," "neurotic," "hysterical"). These derogatory definitions not only distort the perception of the therapist and patient but also imply the irreversibility of psychological disorders and the patient's initial defectiveness. Moreover, they prevent the therapist and patient from concentrating on specific problems and how to solve them. It must be remembered that depressed patients in many situations act quite competently; they are found to be insolvent only in very specific circumstances.

A patient's negative mindset can be a source of irritation for the therapist. Some therapists are tempted to blame the patient for excessive dependence, passivity, "resistance," "lack of will," pessimism, or "unwillingness to cooperate." The frustrated therapist is not able to objectively evaluate the negative ideas of the patient and understand that the above forms of behavior are a logical continuation of distorted thinking.

The most productive approach is to assume that if the patient had a choice (or rather, if he believed in the possibility of choice), he would prefer to be less helpless, more active and independent. If the patient refuses to do homework, misses appointments, or constantly emphasizes his disability, the therapist should look for the cognitive causes that caused this regressive behavior.

Do Not Search for Self-Defeating Behavior of "Unconscious Motives"

The therapist should not give in to the temptation to explain the patient's self-defeating behavior with "infantile desires." Cognitive therapy is based on the belief that the main determinant of the behavior of a depressed patient is his idea of himself, his life situation, and his future. In therapeutic schools that continue the tradition of psychoanalysis, it is believed that the patient's opposition and self-defeating behavior are based on unconscious desires, and that awareness of these desires helps the patient choose more adaptive behavioral strategies. However, this approach seems to us unacceptable when working with depressed patients. The fact is that the latter usually interpret such "insights" as proof of their own "viciousness" or "insignificance" and, as a result, feel even more depressed.

Balance your Own Level of Activity with the Needs of the Patient

A depressed patient has difficulty concentrating. As a result of this, he often cannot even identify the problem, let alone solve it. As a result, whenever a problem arises, he is lost and feels helpless. Due to his negative cognitive attitude, a depressed patient usually sees in the silence of the therapist a sign of rejection, and the absence of precisely specified terms of treatment is regarded as evidence that he will never recover. In light of the foregoing, it is obvious that the method of the unstructured interview cannot be used in the treatment of depressed patients because it provides scope for negative fantasies and interpretations.

Unlike traditional types of psychotherapy, where the patient himself chooses the topic of discussion, and the therapist simply listens to the patient, from time to time reflecting what he heard, the therapist takes a more active position in cognitive therapy and takes more initiative. A cognitive therapist acts as a guide, adviser, educator in the spirit of Socrates, directing the conversation and attention of the patient to specific targets.

Typically, the therapist is most active in the early stages of therapy. He titrates the level of his own activity in accordance with the patient's need for structure. In the deep depression, many patients are not able to give detailed answers; they answer the therapist's questions in one word or a short sentence. In this case, the therapist must be extremely active in order to stir up the patient and remove him from the depressed state. Brief, direct, and specific statements are most effective in this case; moreover, the therapist must seek clear and concrete answers from the patient to their questions.

As depression eases, the therapist lowers his level of activity. It encourages the patient to take the lead in treatment; for example, he may ask the patient to determine the cross-cutting theme of his ideas or to indicate which unspoken assumptions he makes in specific situations. Nevertheless, unlike other therapists, the cognitive therapist remains active throughout the course of treatment and often takes the initiative even in the final stages of therapy.

However, even the most active cognitive therapist pauses after his questions and comments, allowing the patient to collect his thoughts and formulate an answer. The duration of these pauses is set individually for each patient. Pauses should not be too short or too long. If the pause is delayed, this may mean that the patient is confused and needs additional instructions from the therapist. On the other hand, inhibited patients need more time to organize their thoughts and give an answer.

The therapist must carefully balance the degree of their own activity with the needs of the patient. Perhaps no other aspect of cognitive therapy is associated with such a share of risk and does not impose such high demands on the skill of the therapist. Typically, depressed patients have a positive perception of the therapist's activity and his attempts to structure the conversation. The patient may think: "The therapist is talking to me; apparently, he likes me." In addition, structured and focused therapeutic contacts help to overcome the difficulty in concentration that most depressed patients experience. On the other hand, the therapist's overly active and directive position can lead the patient to the idea that the therapist is manipulating him, that he is indifferent to the patient's feelings and desires, that he is more interested in trying out his methods than helping the person.

The Structure of Cognitive Therapy

Prepare the Patient for Therapy

Preparation for cognitive therapy consists of two elements: 1) the patient must understand the principles of the cognitive approach; 2) the patient should be prepared for temporary deterioration of his condition during therapy.

Justification of the cognitive approach. The therapist prepares the patient for therapy, mainly during the first two sessions. The therapist presents the treatment plan to the patient and justifies its use. After that, he explains to the patient what "automatic thoughts" are and what kind of connection exists between thoughts and feelings. He can explain this relationship with a specific example.

Therapist. Man's feelings depend on how he interprets events. I will give you an example. Recently, one of my patients, who successfully completed the treatment, told me about the thoughts that visited her at the beginning of therapy, when she sat in the waiting room, waiting for a meeting with me. She zealously watched what time I started the session. If I was late for at least a few minutes, she thought: "He does not want to see me," and this thought upset her. If I started the session a little earlier than the appointed time, she would say to herself: "My business must be really bad if he is willing to spend extra time on me," and she was worried. In those cases, when I started the session strictly on schedule, she had the thought: "He has a real conveyor here. I'm just another patient for him." And she felt annoyed. As you can see, no matter what time I start the session, she interpreted this in an extremely negative way, and these negative interpretations caused her negative emotions. The patient was able to understand the relationship between her thoughts and feelings. Having learned to identify her thoughts and communicate about them, she realized their irrationality. Now, when she had such thoughts, she could independently correct them, and this led to the disappearance of negative emotions.

During therapy, the therapist constantly draws the patient's attention to how thought is associated with feeling. If the patient says: "I feel terrible," the cognitive therapist will ask: "What are you thinking now?" If the patient writes in his diary that, while doing this or that homework, he felt "oppressed" or "depressed," the therapist asks him to tell what thoughts preceded these unpleasant feelings. You can also ask the patient what this homework means to him.

Studying the possibilities of using the cognitive approach in the treatment of depression, we followed this procedure. After the therapist explained to the patient the goals and objectives of the cognitive approach and justified its application, the patient received the brochure "How to overcome depression" (Beck, Greenberg, 1974). He was invited to read the brochure, emphasizing those places that would raise questions or seem especially important. In essence, this proposal is nothing but the first homework.

This general approach - an explanation of each stage of treatment and each homework - is applied throughout the course of therapy. The therapist tries to make the treatment as clear as possible for the patient so that he can actively participate in determining his own problems and finding ways to solve them.

Recently, we started an experimental study in which patients received a video explaining the goals and characteristics of the cognitive approach. The use of this form of clarification reduced the percentage of cases of incomplete treatment and increased the susceptibility to therapy in poorly educated patients (see Rush and Watkins, 1977). You can also show the patient a video of his own interview to demonstrate the connection between the verbalized idea and the subsequent emotional reaction.

Exacerbations and relapses. It is very important during the first few interviews to find out the patient's expectations regarding the therapy. Some patients expect a miracle, and then, when the miracle does not occur, they experience bitter disappointment. Others, by virtue of a chronically pessimistic outlook on life or having experience of unsuccessful therapy, do not believe in the possibility of healing. As a result of such expectations, they tend to interpret in the most negative way, even the slightest exacerbation of symptoms.

The therapist must explain to the patient that depression is characterized by natural ups and downs in intensity. For example, after several "bright" days, a person's mood may deteriorate sharply. In many patients, even after several weeks of therapy, there are no noticeable improvements. Both the therapist and the patient, counting on success, nevertheless must be prepared to meet exacerbation of symptoms and relapse of depression calmly.

Explain the Treatment Plan to the Patient

The main goals of the cognitive treatment of depression are a) as quickly as possible mitigating depressive symptoms, and b) preventing relapse. To achieve these goals, the patient must learn a) to identify and modify their dysfunctional thoughts and behavior, and b) to recognize and correct cognitive patterns that lead to dysfunctional thinking and behavior. The therapist explains these goals to the patient during the first therapeutic session. The weakening of depressive symptoms implies an increase in feelings of satisfaction and feelings of well-being. When the therapist speaks about this goal to the patient, he may hear a statement like: "I will never be happy unless a friend comes back to me." In this case, the therapist replies: "Regardless of whether a friend returns to you or not, you do not need to suffer as much as you are suffering now." Or he may say: "You are more likely to return your friend if you get out of depression."

The technique of focusing on specific problems deserves a separate discussion. The general and initial goal of therapy - the alleviation of depressive symptoms - can only be achieved by identifying and solving particular problems of the patient. It is important to teach the patient a logical approach to problems and equip him with various techniques that will help him cope with these problems. In other words, the task of cognitive therapy is to help the patient develop certain skills and not just neutralize his suffering. A similar approach is used in behavioral therapy in the treatment of obesity, where the common goal, it would seem, is weight loss. However, the therapist is aimed not so much at losing weight, but at changing attitudes and behavior that lead to obesity. The patient develops specific skills that allow him not only to reduce but also to control his weight constantly.

Similarly, the short-term goal of cognitive therapy - the alleviation of depressive symptoms - is achieved by sequentially identifying the patient's problems and developing appropriate skills. The patient learns: a) to realistically evaluate significant events and situations for him, b) to pay attention to various aspects of situations, c) to produce alternative explanations, and d) to check his maladaptive assumptions and hypotheses by changing behavior and testing more adaptive ways of interacting with the outside world.

The long-term goal of cognitive therapy is to facilitate the process of psychological maturation, which involves honing acquired skills and developing a more objective attitude to reality. In addition, it includes honing interpersonal communication skills and mastering more effective methods of adaptation to complex and diverse situations.

Set an Agenda at the Beginning of the Session

The therapist acts as a guide, guide, providing his ward with a plan, map, and tools. However, he needs to make sure that the patient is ready and wants to follow the plan. Therefore, at the beginning of each meeting, the therapist must, together with the patient, determine which topics should be addressed during this session. To begin with, you should consider how the patient coped with homework. After that, you need to formulate the topics of this session. Topics should be formulated in the form of specific and precise goals. For example, a therapist might say: "So, first, we'll take care of the automatic thoughts that visited you this week and see how you can temper them."

The topic of the interview depends on several factors. Obviously, the first and most important factor is the stage of treatment and the progress the patient has made. The therapist may be interested in whether the patient has learned to recognize and register his maladaptive ideas, whether he is able to independently identify and correct the logical errors made by him, etc.

The second important factor is related to what problems are most worrying for the patient at the moment. The agenda also depends on the severity of the depression. In severe cases, we often use behavioral tasks, and as the depressive symptoms soften, we turn to cognitive tasks that require abstract thinking.

Unresolved issues from the previous session should also be included on the agenda. It is necessary to ask the patient if he has any unresolved problems after the previous session, and if any, they should be worked out at this session.

And finally, the therapist should be attentive to the "secret" concerns of the patient, which the patient does not want to talk about, and which may float out at the end of the session when there is too little time to discuss them.

For all this, the therapist should not be bound by a predetermined sequence of identifying and solving problems because this may prevent him from noticing important current events. It is obvious that an unexpectedly discovered acute problem requires urgent consideration, even to the detriment of some items on the already drawn up agenda. To find out such topics, the "Protocol of Dysfunctional Thoughts," filled out by the patient, and the diary, in which the patient notes what he was doing and what thoughts he visited during the day, help to find such topics.

So, taking into account all of the above requirements, the therapist and patient draw up a session plan. First, the therapist tries to breed and identify different problems. Then he agrees with the patient in what order these problems will be worked out. After that, he can reflect on the means by which each problem should be solved (for example, using role-play, induced images or refutation of automatic thoughts), and discusses with the patient how acceptable these methods are for him. Since the techniques must be selected, taking into account the individual characteristics and needs of the patient, it is desirable that the right of the final decision belongs to the patient.

Engage the Patient's Relatives and Friends

Based on our own therapeutic experience, we believe that the therapeutic effect of an interview can be enhanced by involving someone from the patient's relatives (e.g., spouse) or friends. If there are no obvious contraindications, these "significant others" should be interviewed immediately after the first meeting with the patient. Such an interview allows obtaining additional information about the symptoms of the disease, the patient's functioning level, determining the degree of suicidal risk, etc. Having explained the meaning of the therapeutic procedures and homework to the patient's family or friend, the therapist can instruct them to monitor the observance of the therapeutic regimen. In addition, by engaging the patient's loved ones and securing their support, the therapist thereby neutralizes the possibility of anti-therapeutic behaviors on their part, such as excessive custody, counterproductive offers, grunts, etc. Finally, such an interview reveals problems in the patient's relationship with loved ones who may be one of the factors of depression. In this case, the therapist may come to the conclusion that "family therapy" is necessary.

In some cases, for example, when working with adolescents and the elderly, you can use specially trained assistants who will not only monitor the implementation of homework but also help the patient identify negative thoughts and deal with them.

Use Audio and Video Tools

You can also enhance the effectiveness of therapeutic interviews using various technical means. It is often useful for a patient to listen to an audio recording of a recent interview. Many patients note that viewing the video recording of the session allows one to see firsthand the maladaptation of one's own behavior.

In our work, we also use special audio and video materials illustrating the use of various therapeutic techniques, for example, the technique of recognition of "automatic thoughts" and opposition to them.

Chapter 5

The First Interview

How to Start an Interview

As our experience shows, therapy begins with the patient's first contact with the therapist - it doesn't matter if they communicate by phone or in the therapist's office. As discussed in chapters 2 and 3, the therapist tries to establish a warm, informal relationship with the patient, but does not try to deny the obvious differences in their statuses; he remembers that the patient sees a specialist in him and is waiting for help. Forming a working relationship with the patient, collecting the necessary information, and applying specific techniques of cognitive therapy - all these tasks can be quite easily solved by the therapist during the first interview.

Many therapists prefer to start the interview with the question: "What do you feel now, sitting here?" Quite often, patients say in response that they are anxious or express pessimism. In this case, the therapist must carefully find out what thoughts are hidden behind these unpleasant feelings. The therapist may ask: "Do you remember what you thought on the way here and sitting in the waiting room?" Or: "What did you expect when you met me?"

Even if he simply shares his expectations with the therapist, the patient steps on the path of therapeutic cooperation.

The following record shows how the therapist can begin the first interview.

Therapist - How did you feel today when you came here?

Patient - I was terribly nervous.

T - Have you had any thoughts about me or the upcoming therapy?

P - I was afraid you would think that I am not suitable for your therapy.

T - What other thoughts and feelings visited you?

P - In truth, I felt some hopelessness. You see, I've already visited so many therapists, and my depression is still with me.

T - Tell me, now, sitting here and talking to me, do you still think that I will refuse you treatment?

P - Well, I don't know ... And you won't refuse?

T - No, of course not. But by the example of this your idea, you can trace how negative expectations make you anxious... How do you feel now that you know that you made a mistake in your expectations?

P - I am not as nervous as before. But I still do not let go of fear. I am afraid that you will not be able to help me.

T - I think a little. Later we will return to this feeling of yours and see if you still experience it. In any case, I think that we were able to trace one important pattern. We have found that negative ideas give rise to unpleasant feelings in a person - in your case, anxiety and a sense of hopelessness... How do you feel now?

P - (A little relaxed). Better.

T - Good ... And now try, as briefly as possible, to formulate what I should help you with.

Starting the interview in this way, the therapist achieves several goals: a) helps the patient to relax and involves the patient in a therapeutic relationship; b) receives information about the negative expectations of the patient; c) shows the patient how his thoughts affect his emotional state; d) the patient, being convinced of the possibility of quickly neutralizing unpleasant feelings, receives an incentive to identify and correct his cognitive distortions.

Search for Information

It should be noted that an expertly conducted interview, along with the fact that it provides the therapist with diagnostic data, information about the patient's past and present life, his psychological problems, attitude to treatment and motivation, also allows the patient to take a more objective look at his problems.

In our studies, we try to obtain as much information as possible about the patient before the first interview, which can significantly accelerate the process of clinical diagnosis. To this end, we use a number of questionnaires, in particular, the Depression Scale (Beck, 1967; Beck, 1978). In addition to providing a quick assessment of the severity of the disease, this questionnaire also helps to highlight symptoms that require immediate intervention (for example, suicidal intentions). In addition, the data on negative thoughts obtained with the help of this questionnaire will allow the therapist to detect the patient's central problem (this can be a constant expectation of failure, self-confidence, suicidal tendencies). Another questionnaire we use, "Scale of Hopelessness" (Beck, Weismann, Lester, Trexler, 1974), contains a number of points regarding the patient's negative ideas about their own future.

The necessary information about the features of creative activity and the relationship between negative thoughts and unpleasant feelings of the patient can be obtained from his answers. Of great importance is the preparation of the patient for therapy, which we wrote about in the previous chapter. Most patients are well versed in the conceptual structure of cognitive therapy; however, in order for the patient to fully understand the features of this approach, he needs additional demonstrations using his own problems as an example.

In some cases, especially when the patient has difficulty expressing himself or is completely unaware of psychology, it is useful to provide him with introductory instructions and information materials explaining what depression and cognitive therapy are. In addition, before starting therapy, the therapist can explain to the patient the general treatment plan. This can be done, for example, like this.

"In the course of our first meetings, you and I should determine what problems and difficulties you are experiencing, and will try some ways to overcome them, which, I hope, will bring you relief. We must find out how you react to certain situations and how these reactions affect your well-being. When we thoroughly examine your reactions, we will know how to help you. In the future, we will try other ways to overcome stress, in particular, those that prevent the development of depression. Many of the procedures we use will become clearer to you when you try to complete them. Do you have any questions?"

Studying the possibilities of using the cognitive approach in the treatment of depression, we followed this procedure. After the therapist explained to the patient the goals and objectives of the cognitive approach and justified its application, the patient received the brochure "How to overcome depression" (Beck, Greenberg, 1974). He was invited to read the brochure, emphasizing those places that would raise questions or seem especially important to him. In essence, this proposal is nothing but the first homework.

This general approach - an explanation of each stage of treatment and each homework - is applied throughout the course of therapy. The therapist tries to make the treatment as clear as possible for the patient so that he can actively participate in determining his own problems and finding ways to solve them.

Recently, we started an experimental study in which patients received a video explaining the goals and characteristics of the cognitive approach. The use of this form of clarification reduced the percentage of cases of incomplete treatment and increased the susceptibility to therapy in poorly educated patients (see Rush and

Watkins, 1977). You can also show the patient a video of his own interview to demonstrate the connection between the verbalized idea and the subsequent emotional reaction.

Notes

The amount of information that can be obtained from the patient is almost unlimited; however, the amount of time devoted to therapy and the number of questions addressed to the patient are unlimited. Practical considerations force the therapist to be content with a limited amount of data, extracting the maximum benefit from it. Despite the fact that even after several interviews, the therapist may not have comprehensive information about the patient, it is extremely important to determine the central problems of the patient at the first session and offer an approximate treatment plan. Moreover, the therapist must strive to alleviate the patient's condition by means of probing questions and various therapeutic techniques by the end of the first session. This task is of particular importance when working with suicidal patients who can commit suicide without waiting for the next meeting with the therapist if they do not feel relief after the first interview. In any case, we recommend taking at least an hour and a half to the first interview.

Diagnostic Information

Obviously, the therapist is required to conduct a full diagnostic examination of the patient unless such an examination has been carried out earlier. But even in this case, it is necessary to carefully question the patient in order to confirm the previously made diagnosis. The therapist must remember that depression is a "many-sided" disorder; it can be "smiling," disguised as an organic disease, and organic disorders, in turn, can dress up in the clothes of depression (Beck, 1967).

A history and study of the patient's mental status should not result in a "staccato" rapid-fire interrogation, which, unfortunately, is resorted to in many psychiatric institutions. Questions regarding specific symptoms should be formulated in such a way as to clarify the patient's current life situation and the social context of his psychological disorders. We demonstrate this using the following interview.

Therapist - Tell us what exactly in your emotional state bothers you?

Patient - I'm depressed all the time ... I need to do one job ... I get up early and then hang around all day, unable to force myself to sit down at the papers...

Please note - the therapist is not satisfied with the patient's first response and is in no hurry to ask the next question. Only after receiving enough information, he proceeds to the next question.

Therapist - What kind of work is this?

Patient - Report on archeology ... I am a graduate student.

T - What else bothers you?

P - My mood is spoiled whenever I need to call a girl and arrange a date ... This is such a problem for me.

T - Have you ever been married?

P - No, but I lived with a girl ... We separated three months ago.

T - Is your depression somehow related to this gap?

P - I think so. This upset me so much that I even returned to live with my parents ... Although I hate living with them.

As you can see, the therapist managed to find out not only about the symptoms of the disease but also about stressful factors, the level of education, and the patient's home situation. Note also that, having waited for a pause after the patient's response, the therapist was able to obtain additional information.

Warning

Using pauses requires a balanced approach. Pauses that are too long may be misinterpreted by the patient as a sign of dissatisfaction with the therapist.

Assessment of Mental Status

The therapist is required to be able to assess the current mental status of the patient. In addition, he should be able to determine if the patient has suicidal tendencies quickly. The latter may be indicated, in particular, by the patient expressed a sense of hopelessness.

The therapist must also consider the possibility of "organic" problems, such as brain disorders, physical illnesses that masquerade as depression, mental disability, etc. Since depressive symptoms are sometimes intertwined with other symptoms, and also because depression can only be one of the manifestations of more serious diseases, such as schizophrenia, the therapist needs strong psychiatric diagnosis skills and knowledge of basic somatic diseases.

Note. Already during the first interview, conclusions can be drawn about how much the patient is capable of introspection, whether he is able to evaluate his ideas and life situation objectively, whether he can concentrate on the subject, etc. In addition, the first interview allows one to assess the patient's ability to rapport, his sense of humor, and motivation. Therefore, do not turn the first interview into a "stress resistance test"; the therapist's task is to highlight and mobilize the patient's strengths ("ego strength") in order to formulate an adequate therapy plan.

A Central Complaint as a Symptom is a Target

Usually, a depressed patient reports the most troubling of his problems, not associating them with depression. Meanwhile, these problems, or the central complaints of the patient, may be evidence that he is experiencing depression. The following are the most common complaints of depressed patients.

1. "My brain is being destroyed. Therefore, I want to die. " In fact, the problem was that the patient had difficulty concentrating - a symptom that he mistakenly interpreted as a manifestation of brain disorders.

2. "I want to divorce my husband." The main problem of the patient was related to her tendency to evaluate people and her relations with people exclusively in black and white. She saw in her husband only flaws, and even those were greatly

exaggerated by her. Another component of depression was that she lost her former affection and love for all her loved ones, and she attached particular importance to the loss of feelings towards her husband, believing that she had fallen out of love with him forever. In fact, in a healthy state, she felt quite happy and was satisfied with her relationship with her spouse.

3. "I have no feelings." We have already indicated that depressed patients often complain about the loss of positive feelings - love, joy, pleasure, sense of humor, etc. When describing their condition, some patients say that they feel like a "zombie" or "subhuman." The lack of affective reactions is regarded by them not as a symptom of depression, but as evidence of irreversible personality changes.

4. "I cannot cope with my problems." In this case, the patient, experiencing some interpersonal problems, exaggerated their severity and, at the same time, underestimated her strength. Not believing in her own abilities, the patient avoided problem situations, which, in turn, nourished her negative self-esteem.

5. "I am bad (bad)." In this case, we are dealing with a negative, moralistic assessment of facts typical of depressed patients. The patient saw in her symptoms of depression (lethargy, difficulty concentrating, and loss of love for loved ones) evidence that she was "a lazy egoist who thinks only of herself."

6. "Life is meaningless." Such statements may indicate suicidal thoughts. (See chapter 10.)

Note. Despite the fact that the central complaint is only a manifestation of depression, it should be treated as a problem that can exacerbate depression. Therefore, central complaints should be identified and considered at the very beginning of therapy - preferably in the first session.

The Therapeutic Goals of the First Interview

The main therapeutic goal of the first interview is to alleviate at least some of the symptoms that concern the patient. Obviously, this task is consistent with the needs of the patient, who rely on the relief of suffering, and with the desire of the therapist to help the suffering person. In addition, if the patient sees that the therapist is able to provide real help to him, he naturally begins to trust the therapist and is more willing to get closer and collaborate. The weakening of symptoms in itself encourages the patient, and the positive effect of the "study" of a particular problem stimulates him to complete homework.

In seeking to alleviate the patient's suffering, the therapist should not rely solely on the healing power of rapport, empathy, or promises of a "speedy recovery." Reassurance and persuasion, of course, can lead to temporary relief, but will not help to correct distorted ideas and persistently negative patient forecasts. Moreover, the therapist's unjustified promises will return to him like a boomerang if the patient suddenly feels worse, which is very likely with depression.

The most effective way is to identify the patient's circle of problems and immediately offer him possible solutions. Some of these methods can be tested already during the interview so that at the end of the session, the patient can independently apply them. Any "successful experience" - even the experience of confrontation with the problem and its objective analysis - can increase the patient's self-confidence. In a sense, a therapeutic interview can be seen as a series of "mini-confrontations": the therapist formulates a "task" (asks a question; puts forward a hypothesis), and the patient offers his own solution (answers a question; accepts, rejects or corrects the therapist's hypothesis). If they come to the conclusion that the patient satisfactorily coped with the "tasks" proposed to him, then the whole procedure can be perceived by the patient as a "successful experience" that refutes previous ideas about his own ineptitude and failure. Of course, the therapist must have mastery; tasks (questions) should be formulated so as to push the patient to the "right" answer. Closed questions are more preferred, for example.

Target Symptom Selection

It is hardly possible to accurately predict what problems the patient will encounter during the first interview and to recommend specific approaches in advance. However, generally speaking, in most cases of moderate and severe depression, the focus of the therapeutic intervention should be primarily the target symptoms.

1. Affective symptoms: sadness, longing, lack of satisfaction, apathy, loss of attachment to loved ones, anxiety.

2. Motivational: the desire to escape from life (usually through suicide); flight from "problems" and everyday affairs.

3. Cognitive: difficulties with concentration, memory impairment, cognitive distortions associated with incorrect processing of information.

4. Behavioral: arise from the above symptoms and include passivity (a person can spend days in bed or in an armchair), alienation from people, lethargy, agitation.

5. Physiological or autonomic: sleep disturbances (increase or decrease in sleep duration); impaired appetite (malnutrition or overeating).

The therapist (with the help of the patient) determines what specific symptoms should be the target of therapeutic intervention. In doing so, he is guided by the following questions.

1. What symptoms cause the most suffering to the patient?

2. Which of the observed symptoms are the most "malleable"?

Specific therapeutic intervention techniques are discussed in detail in the next five chapters. In the meantime, we only say that these techniques can be divided into two groups: a) predominantly behavioral, when the impact on the patient's behavior, namely the involvement of the patient in any activity, leads to alleviation of his suffering and mitigation of other, non-behavioral symptoms; b) predominantly cognitive, when therapeutic efforts are directed at changing the patient's thinking.

In mild forms of depression, the focus of attention can be shifted to solving those external problems that provoke the development of depression or exacerbate its course. These may be problems and difficulties that the patient encounters at home, at school, or at work. Often, these problems are caused by loss, for example, a break in relations with a loved one, inability to achieve the desired goal, or to do what you love. The therapist helps the patient to reconsider his attitude to certain things, discusses with him possible ways to overcome a difficult situation and ways to resist stress. In this case, the therapist must remember that situational problems and depression can exacerbate each other. The therapist's task is to make adjustments to this reciprocal relationship in order to alleviate both external stresses and depressive symptoms.

Patient Feedback

In the previous chapter, we already talked about the feedback mechanism and its significance for therapeutic cooperation. By feedback, we mean not only that the therapist observes the patient's emotional reactions, but also the patient's statements indicating his attitude to the therapist and therapy.

A reciprocal feedback system, the therapist and patient exchange impressions, allowing both to make sure that they understand each other correctly, which is especially important in the first interview. This exchange of impressions can proceed as follows.

1. The therapist summarizes what the patient has stated and outlines the main problems.

"So, summing up your story, I can identify three main problems that concern you. First of all, you are alarmed that your son has problems at school. The complaints of the teachers upset you so much that you were unable to understand what caused your son's bad behavior and somehow help him. The second problem is related to your husband. He began to linger often from work, and you assume that he started an affair on the side. You do not discuss this topic with him, because you are afraid that he will confirm your assumptions. In addition, it bothers you that he is annoyed when you ask him to return home early... Am I right? Well ... And finally, the third problem is that you have stopped monitoring yourself and are now disgusted with yourself. You've gotten very well and can't pull yourself together, as they say ... Tell me, did I list your problems correctly? "

The patient can amend or supplement the therapist's resume. Typically, the patient is pleased when the therapist accurately summarizes his words. Firstly, it gives him the feeling that he is understood, and secondly, he sees that the situation, which seemed to him confusing and hopeless, can be broken down into a number of particular problems that are quite amenable to solution.

2. To make sure that the patient perceives the conceptualizations proposed to him, you need to ask him to state how he understood the therapist's words. Here is what the patient responded to the therapist's summary above:

"Now, I understand that I noticed only the wrong behavior of Johnny. I was so tormented by the thought that he would grow up to be a bad person, and I was so angry with him that I didn't even try to find out what really happened there. I need to talk with both the teacher and Johnny himself ... If I understood correctly, you advise me to stop scolding my husband when he comes home late. Yes, I think we need to start with this, and then, perhaps, I can directly ask him if he has another woman. In the meantime, I need to try to get out of depression. If I take care of myself, I become more attractive; it will be easier for me to solve the problem with my husband. "

In this case, the patient not only accepted the conclusions of the therapist but also suggested possible solutions to the problems.

3. The third type of feedback we mentioned above. The therapist is trying to find out if the interview causes counterproductive reactions in the patient. If the therapist feels that they and the patient are "treading water," he should ask what the patient is thinking.

In any case, at the end of the session, it is useful to ask the patient about his attitude to the interview in order to prevent the development of "delayed" negative reactions. The therapist may, for example, ask: "We have covered quite a few topics with you. Were there moments when some of my words seemed offensive or unpleasant to you? Maybe something was incomprehensible to you? Have we missed something important? "With such inquiries, it may turn out that the patient misinterpreted or did not fully understand some of the therapist's statements.

4. In the same way, having entrusted the patient with some task, the therapist may ask: "How do you like this task? Would you like to try to fulfill it, or does it seem burdensome to you? "Only after giving the patient the opportunity to choose, the therapist has the right to count on a sincere answer.

5. Finally, it is necessary to find out how the patient responded to the previous interview. Since patients tend to inform the therapist more likely of a positive attitude towards interviews and homework and to conceal negative reactions, the latter requires particularly careful research.

Chapter 6

Behavioral Techniques

Cognitive Modification through Behavioral Changes

Cognitive therapy for depression is based on the cognitive theory of depression. Working within the framework of the cognitive model, the therapist chooses specific approaches that correspond to the current needs of a particular patient. The therapist can rely on cognitive theory, even using purely behavioral or reactive (release of emotions) techniques.

At the initial stages of therapy, and especially in cases of severe depression, the cognitive therapist often faces the task of restoring the premorbid level of patient functioning. Using various means, the therapist encourages the patient to overcome his passivity and do something constructive. The validity of this approach is confirmed by numerous clinical observations. The fact is that the inactivity of a depressed person makes him and his relatives ("significant others") believe that he is no longer able to perform the functions associated with his social role (student, earner, hostess, spouse, parent, etc.). P.). Moreover, the patient no longer expects to enjoy the activities that were once interesting to him.

We observe a kind of vicious circle here: inactivity gives rise to thoughts of incapacity, which, in turn, cause even greater depression and massive motor inhibition up to complete immobility. Intelligent operations, such as pondering and planning motor activity, present a problem for a deeply depressed patient, not to mention complex motor operations that require tremendous effort. Violation of these behaviors as a result of decreased attention increased fatigue, or emotional depression leads to a feeling of dissatisfaction and a decrease in self-esteem.

The role of the therapist is clear. However, it must be remembered that it is not so easy to "dissuade" a patient who sincerely considers himself weak, insolvent, or lazy. After all, the patient knows that he does not do what once seemed important to him and was given without much effort. By helping the patient change behavior, the therapist thereby demonstrates the fallacy of the above negative generalized conclusions. The therapist can show the patient that he has not lost the ability to function normally, that only despondency and pessimism do not allow him to mobilize his resources and make the necessary efforts. Thus, he leads the patient to the realization that the source of his problems are cognitive errors: the patient thinks (erroneously) that he is weak, incapable, stupid, and these prejudices limit his motivation and behavior.

The term "behavioral techniques" seems to indicate that the object of therapeutic intervention is only behavior, that the therapist simply prescribes certain types of activity to the patient. In fact, for the successful application of behavioral methods, constant attention to the thoughts, feelings, and desires of the patient is necessary. The ultimate goal of behavioral techniques in the framework of cognitive therapy is to change negative attitudes that interfere with the normal functioning of the patient. The therapist using these techniques, in fact, conducts a series of experiments designed to refute the patient's negative ideas about his person. Obtaining clear evidence of the fallacy of his ideas, the patient gradually becomes more self-confident and takes on the implementation of more complex tasks.

Many of the techniques described in this chapter are part of the arsenal of behavioral therapy. However, the effect of therapy based only on the behavioral model is usually small, since the therapist focuses only on the patient's external behavior, excluding from consideration his cognitive background, namely hidden attitudes, beliefs, and thoughts of the patient. For a behavioral therapist, behavioral change is an end in itself, while in cognitive therapy, it serves only as a means to an end - cognitive modification.

It is important to note that behavioral changes do not necessarily lead to cognitive adjustment. In contrast to the results of socio-psychological studies of healthy people, our observations show that depressed patients, even changing their behavior, do not always abandon their overvalued negative ideas. We illustrate this point with the following example.

The 36-year-old woman, depressed, stopped attending a tennis club, although previously she enjoyed tennis a lot. Now, by her confession, she just did" that she was sleeping or trying to "do something around the house." The patient firmly held the opinion that she was not capable of such "intense" activities as tennis. The patient's husband, wanting to help his wife overcome depression, agreed with the instructor about private tennis lessons. The patient reluctantly went to the lesson, and there, according to her husband, "changed": her blows were accurate and accurate; the reaction was agile. However, despite the successes, the patient concluded that the previous skills were "irretrievably lost," and no lessons would help return them. Her husband's positive reaction was interpreted by her as proof of her ineptitude: "He believes that without these lessons, I won't be able to hit the ball." Obviously, this interpretation had no real basis for itself but stemmed from a negative assessment of their own abilities. The patient said that she did not get any pleasure from the lesson, explaining that she, as they say, "does not deserve" entertainment.

This case clearly indicates that the significance of behavioral changes cannot be overestimated. Changes in behavior do not necessarily entail a rejection of negative prejudices - rather, they open up the possibility of reassessing previously formed attitudes and beliefs. Behavioral changes are important to the extent that they allow the patient to test their ideas of incompetence and inadequacy empirically. Therefore, the use of behavioral techniques should be based on a clear understanding of the patient's belief system. In this example, the patient's husband, although he outlined the right course of action (tennis lessons), could not help her solve the cognitive problem, because he was thinking in a completely different coordinate system. Moreover, his efforts led to the opposite results - the patient saw in this undertaking yet another proof of her inferiority.

Drawing Up the Daily Routine

According to the evidence of many depressed patients, their pessimistic thoughts and self-deprecating assessments become especially acute in periods of physical and social passivity. Patients, scolding themselves for their inactive, "plant" existence and distance from people, at the same time justify their inaction and self-isolation by the imaginary senselessness of social contacts or unwillingness to be a burden to others. In addition, this passive existence once again convinces them of their own inferiority and failure, and the vicious circle closes.

The therapeutic technique, which provides for the preparation of an action plan for the patient, is based on clinical observations that indicate that depressed people find it difficult to complete tasks that they can easily cope with in a healthy state. A depressed patient is inclined to avoid complex tasks, and if he undertakes them, then, as a rule, he experiences difficulties in their implementation and is in a hurry to capitulate. Statements such as "Why try in vain?" Or "Everything is meaningless," speak of the patient's disbelief in his own strength.

The technique of action planning is used to increase the patient's motivation, encourage him to be more active, and distract from gloomy thoughts. In addition, by involving the patient in a focused activity, the therapist receives objective information about his functional capabilities.

The use of this technique, as well as other techniques of cognitive therapy, requires justification. Many patients realize that inactivity contributes to dysphoria and gloomy meditation and ultimately exacerbates their suffering. The therapist may suggest that the patient "conduct an experiment" to check if his mood improves if he engages in any purposeful activity. They jointly outline what the patient should do during the day, and then the therapist instructs the patient to monitor their thoughts and feelings during these tasks. If the patient stubbornly refuses the experiment, you can directly ask him: "What will you lose if you try?"

The technique allows for flexible use. The patient can be guided by a predefined daily routine, or can simply note in the diary what he did during the day. This technique can be used in conjunction with the graded assignment technique.

Assessment of Skill and Pleasure

Many depressed patients, even supporting a fairly active lifestyle, do not receive satisfaction from their studies. This inability to enjoy activities can be explained by the following reasons: a) a person tries to do things that never gave him pleasure; b) negative ideas dominating consciousness take precedence over a potential sense of pleasure; c) the extreme selectivity of perception and thinking makes a depressed person inattentive to the feeling of pleasure.

In the first case, patients initially take on not too pleasant work, such as housework, and as a result, even after successfully coping with it, they do not feel satisfied. The patient either rejects the activities that give him pleasure or cannot remember what he had previously enjoyed. The therapist is faced with the task of finding out why the patient is not doing business that is pleasant for him. A typical explanation often heard from depressed patients is: "I do not deserve pleasure because I am not doing anything useful." To overcome this way of thinking, the therapist must explain that a sense of pleasure helps a person, even if only temporarily, to improve their mood.

Special questionnaires allow the therapist to evaluate what classes can please the patient. Having chosen any potentially pleasant occupation, the therapist asks the patient to engage in this business daily for a certain period and note all changes in mood. If various activities are included in the daily routine, it is useful to ask the patient to evaluate each activity in terms of skill (M) and pleasure (Y) (see the section on preparing the daily routine). By the term "skill," we mean a feeling of satisfaction with our own results, and by "pleasure," we mean any pleasant feelings associated with a specific form of activity. The degree of skill and pleasure can be evaluated on a five-point scale: a rating of "0" means that the lesson did not give the patient any satisfaction (pleasure), and a rating of "5" means the maximum degree of satisfaction (pleasure). Using this scale, the patient learns to recognize his small achievements and becomes more attentive to the feeling of pleasure. This technique allows you to overcome the categorical thinking of the patient, the tendency to assess the situation on the principle of "all or nothing."

It is very important to correctly explain the concepts of skill and pleasure to the patient. "Mastery" is not necessarily related to the degree of difficulty or the complete completion of the task. Many patients, evaluating the degree of mastery, compare the quality of their current performance with their past achievements. For example, a patient can say: "It's the same for me - to call a friend! I used to make ten calls per day and did not attach any importance to this." Or: "What about the fact that I did something around the house? It is natural. I have to do it." The therapist explains to the patient that in assessing the degree of skill, he should proceed from his current state, and not from ideal ideas that in depression even the simplest things sometimes seem like a "burden" to a person, and therefore even a small step in the direction of the goal should be considered an achievement.

The concept of pleasure includes feelings such as joy, pleasure, fun, interest. Mastery and pleasure can act as independent, independent of each other categories. Even if the patient does not feel any pleasure from the lesson, you need to encourage him to an objective assessment of the level of his own skill. Often a rating of "O" on a scale of pleasure or skill after a successfully completed task is sometimes associated with a negative interpretation of the event. For example, one of our patients noted that he did not enjoy reading newspapers, whereas, in the past, this was his favorite pastime. When asked by the therapist what he was thinking about reading the newspapers, the patient replied: "I remembered how I lost my job. When you read these articles, it seems that the world is going to collapse." In the same way, the patient appreciated his mastery. He believed that he could not cope with the task (washing the car), because "he could not achieve perfect whiteness and could not force himself to vacuum the interior." Concentrating on what was not done, the patient lost sight of what he was able to do. The therapist explained to the patient that thinking on the principle of "all or nothing" prevents him from objectively evaluating his abilities and achievements.

Along with the fact that the patient has the opportunity to understand what classes give him pleasure and replace unpleasant duties with more pleasant things, the planning technique of the day, combined with an assessment of skill and pleasure, allows the therapist to identify and correct the patient's cognitive distortions. We demonstrate this with a concrete example.

Here is an excerpt from the diary of a 38-year-old patient, an administrator who was undergoing cognitive therapy in connection with depression.

Saturday M U

8.00-9.00 I woke up, got dressed, had breakfast

9.00-12.00 Glued wallpaper in the kitchen

12.00-13.00 Lunch

13.00-15.00 I watched TV

Judging by the estimates, the rise and breakfast brought the patient some pleasure, and all other classes did not bring either satisfaction or pleasure. Meanwhile, the patient, despite the depression, made repairs in the kitchen. What prevented him from properly assessing his achievement?

Therapist. Why didn't you rate the success of wallpapering your kitchen as a successful experience?

Patient. Because I stuck badly, in many places, flowers do not dock.

T. But you brought the matter to an end?

P. Yes.

T. Is this your kitchen?

P. No. I helped a neighbor.

T. That is, most of the work was done by a neighbor? (The therapist, in this case, is trying to figure out what other reasons made the patient devalue his achievement.)

P. No. In fact, I glued, and he was in the wings. He never had to glue wallpaper.

T., I see. What else was wrong? Maybe you spilled a paste, or spoiled the wallpaper, or left a mess after yourself?

P. Yes, no. The only trouble is that it was not always possible to dock the pattern.

T. So, you do not consider this an achievement only because the work is not perfect?

P. Well ... yes.

T. And how big are the differences in the pattern?

P. (shows with fingers a distance of approximately 0.5 cm). Something like that.

T. Are the differences at all junctions?

P. No ... only on two or three.

T. How many?

P. In total, there were about twenty to twenty-five bands.

T. Has anyone else noticed these inconsistencies?

P. No. A neighbor, for example, believes that everything turned out fine.

T. And your wife? Did she see your work?

P. Yes. She liked it.

T. Tell me, are these flaws noticeable if you step back a few steps from the wall and look at it as a whole?

P. No ... I don't think so.

T. It turns out that you notice only flaws in your work. Tell me, is it wise to completely depreciate your results based on a few tiny defects?

P. But I could stick better.

T. Imagine that the kitchen was not pasted over by you, but by the neighbor himself. What would you tell him?

P. Hm ... Great job!

As you can see, the therapist first found out in detail what the patient was doing. After that, he tried to identify the discrepancies between the real achievements and feelings of the patient. Then, through careful questioning, the therapist established the causes of these discrepancies and found out on what facts the patient's conclusions are based ("Flowers did not dock"). These facts were subjected to an objective analysis, which included: 1) a comparison of one fact with others (the patient did most of the work; no one noticed flaws) and 2) an assessment of the facts from different perspectives ("What would you say if you didn't paste the kitchen, and the neighbor himself?").

The Technique of Graduated Tasks

Usually, after a series of tasks are successfully completed, depressed patients experience some (even short-term) increase in mood and motivation. The patient feels that he is able to cope with more complex tasks - of course, provided that he overcomes his inherent tendency to belittle his achievements.

An example of graded assignments is described by Goldfried (in one of his letters, 1974), who independently discovered this technique. It is curious that the technique he invented is based on the same principles that our group used. Dr. Goldfried writes:

"Based on the assumption that depression arose as a result of her (patient's) imaginary inability to control her living space, I instructed her to perform a number of specific tasks (to make up her bed in the morning, get dressed, and clean the rooms) to show that she is actually quite capable of controlling the world around her.

When she learned to cope with these simplest tasks, I entrusted her with more complex things. An important point in therapy was that I constantly forced her to "step back" to evaluate the results and understand what changes had occurred in her life as a result of these efforts."

The technique of graduated tasks consists of the following key points.

1. Definition of the problem (such may be, for example, the patient's conviction that he is not able to achieve vital goals).

2. Project development. Step-by-step organization of tasks (or classes) from simple to more complex.

3. Performing a specific task, the patient sees that he can achieve his goal, thereby refuting his belief in his own incompetence.

4. Clarification and discussion of the patient's doubts, overcoming skepticism, and a tendency to diminish their achievements.

5. The therapist encourages the patient to a realistic, objective assessment of the results.

6. A constant emphasis on the fact that the patient achieved his goal thanks to his efforts and skills.

7. Development of new, more complex tasks.

We illustrate the application of this technique with a concrete example from practice.

The therapist visited a 40-year-old depressed patient on the first day of her hospitalization. Despite the persuasion of the ward nurse, the woman did not want to do anything and lay in bed, thinking about her problems and feeling more and more miserable. She believed that nothing could please her.

The patient admitted to the therapist that before the illness, she enjoyed reading. She said: "I have not read anything in the last two months. Now I'm not able to read the headline in the newspaper." However, despite her doubts, she agreed to try reading a few lines. The therapist took a storybook from the hospital library and suggested that the patient read the shortest one in his presence. "I cannot read," the patient said. - The therapist replied: "Try to read the first paragraph aloud." "But these will be just words," the woman objected. "I cannot concentrate on the content." "Let's try," the therapist suggested. "Read the first sentence aloud."

The patient read the first sentence and continued reading until she reached the end of the paragraph. The therapist told her to read further, but not aloud, but to herself. The story so fascinated the patient that she did not notice how she turned the page. The therapist said that he should go away for a while and asked the woman to continue reading. About an hour later, a psychiatrist called him and said: "I just saw a patient who, for some reason you think is depressed." Returning to the ward, the therapist found that the patient's mood had really improved. The patient was instructed to read one story daily. By the end of the week, the patient had read the entire collection and started the novel, and on the tenth day of hospitalization, her condition was found to be satisfactory, and the patient returned home.

A depressed patient, as a rule, believes that he is not able to fulfill the task given to him or that he is not at all able to do anything. Therefore, the therapist must break the task into pieces and begin with offer the patient something that he will surely cope with. After the patient has successfully completed several elementary tasks during the therapeutic session, he receives "homework," each time more complex, for example, from boiling eggs to preparing dinner.

It is very important to compare the degree of difficulty of the task with the real capabilities of the patient because any failure will be interpreted by the patient as evidence of his inferiority. That is why we recommend that therapists first try out the technique during the session and only then give the patient homework. The therapist can offer the patient to try to complete one or another task, not for the sake of the final result, but in order to find out how much he is actually able to do: "Even if you do not succeed in this endeavor, we will receive important information about your condition." In this context, even "failures" have a positive meaning, because they serve as a source of information in the development of subsequent projects.

Another typical mistake when using the graded assignment technique is that therapists sometimes forget to find out how the patient himself evaluates his results. Depressed patients, even quite successfully coping with assigned tasks, tend to belittle or devalue their achievements. A patient, for example, may think: "I would have spent half as much time on this as I am now" or "What is it that I did this?" Depression still didn't go away."

The therapist must "draw out" all these reservations and negations from the patient and refute them. The first objection can be refuted as follows: "We were faced with the task of checking whether you can do this or not. You claimed you couldn't. But you could, you did it. The fact that you worked with less productivity than before is a completely different problem." In response to the second objection, the therapist can give the patient the following explanations: "We did not expect an instant decrease in depression, we did not even set ourselves such a task. We took this initiative to check if you are right, believing that you do not cope with the task. What do you think now - were you right? This quest is just the first step to defeating depression. The disease will not go away until we complete the entire sequence of steps. However, your well-being and mood will depend on whether you remain optimistic and how objectively evaluate your achievements."

Cognitive Rehearsal

One of the problems that arise in the treatment of depressed patients is that in depression, a person is sometimes not able to perform even the most mundane, familiar actions that he had previously performed without hesitation, almost automatically. A number of psychological factors, such as distraction, inability to concentrate, etc., may limit the behavioral repertoire of a depressed patient. For example, a person goes to the kitchen to drink water and forgets why he came there. Such episodes, repeating, again and again, give rise to fear in a person: he begins to think that he has a brain disease that threatens dementia.

"Cognitive rehearsal" is nothing more than mental reproduction by the patient of the whole sequence of steps necessary for the successful completion of a specific task. This procedure serves as an effective antidote to absent-mindedness because it makes the patient focus on the task.

The technique is also used to identify potential "barriers" (cognitive, behavioral, and environmental) that may arise when performing certain actions. The central task of the therapist is to identify these problems and suggest ways to solve them in order to prevent an unwanted feeling of failure. It is significant that the mere mental execution of a task sometimes improves the patient's well-being.

Here is an example of identifying psychological barriers using the technique of cognitive rehearsal.

The patient, a 24-year-old housewife, agreed to continue aerobics classes.

Therapist. So, you agree that you should try aerobics again.
Patient Yes. I always felt so good after these classes.

T. Okay, then I will ask you to connect your imagination. Imagine going to class. What are you going to do?
P. Well, just get in the car and drive.

T. No, more specifically, please. We know that you have already made the decision to resume classes more than once, but each time there were some obstacles. Now you need to describe your actions in detail and tell what you feel and what you think about when you are going to classes.

P. Ah, I see.

T. So, classes begin at nine in the morning. What time do we start?

P. At half-past seven ... At seven to thirty, the alarm will ring. I will wake up, and I will probably have a lousy mood. It's always hard for me to get up in the morning.

T. And how do you overcome this difficulty?

P. I'll lie down for ten minutes until I come to my senses. Then I get up, get dressed, and have breakfast. After breakfast, I'll start to pack up ... (Pause.) Oh, wait! I have no shorts! Here it is, an obstacle.

T. What can you do to solve this problem?

P. Well, I can run to the store and buy some.

T. Do it mentally ... What's next?

P. Further ... I am ready to go, but I discover that there is no car.

T. How can this obstacle be overcome?

P. I'll ask my husband to adjust the car in advance.

T. What do you imagine now?

P. Imagine going to class, but halfway around, I turn around and go back.

T. Why?

P. Because I suddenly thought that I would look like an idiot there.

T. What do you say to yourself in response to this thought?

P. I'll say that people come there to do aerobics, and not to laugh at each other.

Assertiveness training and role-playing games

The technique of conducting an assertive training is described in detail in numerous methodological manuals. Generally speaking, assertiveness training is aimed at developing a person's ability to assert his rights and includes techniques such as modeling and behavioral rehearsal. Data on the effectiveness of the entire procedure and its individual components are presented in the relevant literature (McFall, Twenty man, 1973).

Role-playing games involve "playing" various situations with the implementation of social interactions in accordance with the selected roles. Assertiveness training and role-playing can be of great help in treating depression. Like other behavioral techniques used in the context of cognitive therapy, these methods are used to identify and overcome dysfunctional ideas and beliefs of the patient.

A 20-year-old depressive patient told the therapist about her "humiliating episode" she had recently experienced, when she, paying for purchases in a department store, was so excited that she could not calculate the required amount. The patient was worried that the cashier must have mistaken her "for an idiot." "I'm so clumsy, so stupid," she repeated. The therapist asked the patient to put herself in the place of the cashier and evaluate the situation from this new position.

Patient (as a cashier). I see that a woman is very confused by her awkwardness. I try to calm her; I say: "It's okay. Everyone can make a mistake."

Therapist. Do you think it is possible that the cashier saw what you see now - well, except that she did not console you?

P. It would be strange if she began to console me. No, she wasn't so sensitive ... I know how it feels to be a fool, so I can put myself in the place of another.

T. Why do you think that the cashier did not react with understanding to your mistake? Did she tell you something? Or looked displeased?

P. No, she patiently waited for me to count the money. She even smiled at me, but from this, I felt like around fool.

T. Well, as far as I understand, we do not have enough data to judge her reaction with confidence. So, let's better discuss now your tendency to perceive yourself as a "fool" when you make mistakes. And then, we will rehearse what line of behavior you could choose if the cashier were really critical.

Role-playing games can also be used to cause the patient to "auto sympathetic." In this case, the therapist and the patient simply change roles. Usually, depressed patients are more demanding and critical of themselves than others who find themselves in the same situation.

An essential aspect of cognitive therapy is the evaluation of perceptions that interfere with assertive behavior. The timid, uncertain behavior characteristic of depressed patients is often explained not so much by a lack of behavioral skills as by the presence of negative prejudices.

Patient X., a 29-year-old man, decided to continue his studies at the university after a ten-year hiatus, during which he worked at the factory. At one of the sessions, he complained to the therapist about the behavior of his 20-year-old fellow student, with whom he shared his workplace in the laboratory. The young student never washed tubes and flasks with him and constantly left the table uncleaned. The patient had a very clear idea of how this problem could be discussed with a comrade, but he always put off the conversation. The therapist tried to find out what thoughts prevented the patient from showing the necessary perseverance.

A patient. You see, I know what to say and how to say it, but every time I am stopped by the thought, "He may think that I am finding fault."

Therapist. And what conclusion can he draw?

P. Probably, he will consider me an inert, conservative type.

T. Are you really an "inert, conservative type"?

P. Yes, no. You know what? I'm just afraid that he will start to intrigue me and that I will have even greater troubles.

It is clear that the patient put off the conversation out of a desire to avoid "trouble." The lack of assertiveness led to the fact that the patient, unsure of the correctness of his decision to return to university, began to experience even greater doubts about this. After the therapist helped the patient weigh the pros and cons, he decided to talk with a friend and easily coped with this task.

General Guidelines for the Use of Behavioral Techniques

When using behavioral techniques, it is important to explain to the patient why he is given a task. The difficulty with working with depressed patients is, in particular, in that they distort post assignment assignments. The therapist must create the conditions for the patient to interpret the results of the assignment within the framework of the original goal. In other words, the original goal should be clear from the start.

Explaining the essence of the task to the patient and evaluating the results, try to avoid generalized statements, so that the patient does not have the illusion that the performance of a single task leads to a complete and final recovery. In this case, it is enough to emphasize that the patient is "moving in the right direction." Of course, positive expectations are a necessary component of success, but it is important to warn the patient about the inadmissibility of an absolutist assessment ("all or nothing") of the results of the task.

The development and implementation of behavioral projects can take place with the participation of "significant others" (spouse, relatives, friends of the patient). These people not only provide moral support to the patient but can also act as an important link in the feedback system.

Some patients, after the successful completion of one task, sharply increase their activity. Although this result is generally desirable, it is fraught with adverse consequences: the patient may overestimate his strength and be defeated when performing more complex tasks. In such cases, it is useful to remind the patient that no one requires grandiose achievements from him, that the initial goals of therapy are to check his negative ideas and gradually increase activity.

As noted earlier, most behavioral techniques are used during the first therapeutic sessions to relieve symptoms such as passivity, lack of satisfaction, and the inability to express emotions. These symptoms are found in almost all depressed patients, but behavioral techniques are especially indicated in cases of severe depression. It is difficult for a deeply depressed patient to concentrate on abstract conceptualizations; the range of his attention is limited and can cover only clearly defined specific tasks. Research in this area shows that successful experience with specific behavioral tasks rather than anything else helps break the vicious circle of demoralization, passivity, and self-abasement. Homework should also be proportionate to the patient's level of understanding. Generally speaking, we do not recommend giving the patient homework at the initial stages of therapy until a similar form of the task is worked out at the session. However, it is not always possible to follow this rule, since many tasks can only be performed in a natural environment (at home, at work, etc.). Cognitive rehearsals and telephone consultations help overcome this problem. It can be agreed that the patient will call the therapist if he has difficulty completing the task. This practice allows the patient to identify and solve problems "on the spot" in a real situation and encourages him to complete the task.

The transition from behavioral to "purely" cognitive methods is possible only when the patient understands the importance of behavioral changes and fully masters behavioral techniques. If behavioral symptoms and problems reoccur, the patient may need a "follow-up course" of behavioral therapy. Summarizing the above, let us say that behavioral techniques are useful to the extent that they help increase the patient's functioning level, neutralize his obsessive thoughts and dysfunctional attitudes, and allow him to experience a sense of satisfaction. Changes in the patient's behavior can shake his negative self-concept, and a revision of the self-concept leads, in turn, to increase motivation and improve mood.

Chapter 7

Cognitive Techniques

Justification

As indicated earlier, the use of cognitive methods requires the therapist to be careful and accurately assess the patient's condition. A depressed patient can be so absorbed in negative thoughts that further introspection will only strengthen his perseverative tendencies. Work with the cognitive components of depression should begin only after the patient is involved in a constructive, focused activity. Of course, if the therapist believes that the patient is initially ready to study his thoughts, feelings, and desires, introspective techniques can be applied already in the first sessions. The early use of cognitive strategies is also shown when working with suicidal patients. However, in the vast majority of cases, a combination of behavioral and cognitive methods is necessary.

Cognitive techniques open access to the patient's cognitive organization. The therapist asks the patient questions in order to identify illogical conclusions and determine on the basis of what principles the patient structures reality. Since the therapist proceeds from his own theory, he must formulate questions in such a way that he does not "put into the mouth" of the patient his own ideas and concepts. Guiding questions should be avoided, as well as the degree of suggestibility of the patient and the inherent desire of some patients to guess the "correct" answer.

Applying cognitive techniques, the therapist must work within the framework of the cognitive theory of depression. As stated in Chapter 1, the reductionist view of cognitive therapy as a rigidly defined series of standard steps, such as typing pa in a waltz or tango, is fundamentally wrong. Cognitive therapy is a harmonious system of procedures aimed at researching and modifying the patient's "personal paradigm." In order for the therapist to be able to penetrate into the patient's inner world and understand the methods used for structuring reality, he must collect adequate information, that is, identify idiosyncratic patterns of patient's thinking and perception.

In a joint study of the inner life and the consistent identification of idiosyncratic ways of constructing reality, the patient often rethinks the meaning of various events. Thus, life takes on a "new meaning" for him. The patient discovers what is preventing him from achieving his desired goals and develops ways to overcome or circumvent these obstacles.

Preparing the Patient for Cognitive Therapy

The therapist first examines how the patient identifies and solves his psychological problems. To correct dysfunctional or distorted perceptions associated with problem areas, the therapist briefly tells the patient about the cognitive model of depression. He explains how a person's ideas about himself, his future, and the world around him (the cognitive triad) affect his feelings, motivation, and behavior. The therapist emphasizes that feeling unwell is the result of a negative way of thinking. However, the therapist must be careful in his statements. For example, one should not call the patient's thinking "irrational." Depressed patients sincerely believe that they see things in their "true light." The therapist must show the patient that his depression is largely determined by his thoughts and perceptions and that the latter may be "not entirely accurate." So, for example, you can demonstrate to the patient the fact that of all the possible interpretations of the event, he systematically selects the most negative ones.

It is important to find out the patient's expectations regarding therapy. We illustrate this point with a concrete example. One of us had to deal with a patient who had previously been unsuccessfully treated three times with various antidepressants. The patient was told that her depression arose as a result of biochemical disorders, and she was firmly convinced that her case was hopeless. Obviously, this particular patient needed information about "Colloquial" therapy - its theoretical foundations, differences from pharmacotherapy, and degree of effectiveness.

A patient who associates his depression with childhood injuries and considers it necessary to recall, "live" again and analyze the events that took place in his childhood, also needs to be reoriented to cognitive therapy. In this case, it is useful to discuss with the patient the possibility of changing the thinking and behavior of a person without analyzing the experience of previous learning.

We illustrate this idea with such an analogy. Imagine a person whose speech is replete with grammatical errors and slang words. To teach him to speak correctly, there is no need to analyze his past learning experience. It is clear that this person needs to undergo additional training, which would include correcting grammatical errors and expanding vocabulary.

The patient's expectations can be identified along the way with an explanation of the conceptual model of cognitive therapy using special brochures ("How to overcome depression," "Cognitive therapy and emotional disorders"). The therapist asks the patient to emphasize those provisions that, in his opinion, are relevant to his case.

The following conversation recording shows how the therapist and patient can examine the subjective significance of events. The patient, a 26-year-old graduate student, had recurrent depression, and the last exacerbation lasted four months.

Patient, I agree with your description, but I cannot agree that my depression is the result of my thinking.

Therapist. What do you think?

P. I get depressed when something doesn't work out for me. For example, when I fail a test.

T. Why is the failure to test so depressing you?

P. If I fail the test, I will not go to law school.

T. I understand that failing a test means a lot to you. But do not think that this event in itself caused depression, because then any person who failed the test would certainly fall into depression. How many people are so oppressed by failure and in need of treatment?

P. It all depends on how important the test is for a person.

T. And who defines this importance?

P. I.

T. So, we have to examine your attitude towards the test (or your thoughts in connection with this test). Do you agree?

P. Yes.

T. Do you agree that your mood and well-being will depend on how you interpret the test results? You may feel depressed; your sleep may be disturbed; your appetite will disappear. Perhaps even you decide to drop out.

P. Yes, I had such thoughts.

T. And what does failure of the test mean for you?

P. (with tears). That I will not enter law school.

T. And what does non-admission to the law faculty mean to you?

P. That I do not have enough mind.

T. What else?

P. That I will never be happy.

T. And how do these thoughts affect your well-being?

P., I feel miserable.

T. So you feel unhappy because you think you will be unhappy if you fail the test. Thus, you are driving yourself into a trap: for you, non-admission to the law faculty means "I will never be happy."

A critical aspect of cognitive therapy is teaching the patient how to observe their cognitions. This training involves the following sequence of steps: 1) explain to the patient what the term cognition means; 2) demonstrate on concrete examples the relationship between cognition and emotions (or behavior); 3) demonstrate the presence of cognition in recent experiences of the patient; 4) as a homework assign the patient to record thoughts; 5) review and discuss with the patient his records.

Clarification of the Term "Cognition"

The therapist can offer the patient the following definition: "Cognition is a thought or figurative representation that may go unnoticed by you if you do not concentrate on them." Typical cognitions characteristic of depression and other clinical disorders are often referred to as "automatic thoughts." It is human nature to believe that his thoughts and ideas are a reflection of reality, and he rarely evaluates their reliability. A depressive patient is filled with rhetorical questions ("Why am I so weak?", "Why can't I do anything?") And unpleasant images ("I am ugly like a pig"), taking for granted that he is a weak, incapable, worthless person.

The Effect of Cognition on Emotions and Behavior

There are a number of ways to demonstrate the relationship between thinking, emotions, and behavior. This relationship can be explained to the patient using an abstract sketch that does not affect him personally.

Therapist. The feelings and behavior of a person depend on how he perceives and interprets events. Imagine: late evening, a man sits in the house alone and suddenly hears some kind of rumble in the next room. He thinks: "There is a robber." What will be his emotions?

Patient He will be alarmed, scared.

T. What do you think he will do?
P. Perhaps he will hide, or perhaps he will be able to call the police.

T. Good. So, the thought of a robber will cause alarm about him and make him take some actions to protect himself. Now imagine that when you hear the same noise, a person thinks: "They forgot to close the window, and something fell to the floor from the wind." What will he feel in this case?
P. Well, I don't know. But certainly not fear. Maybe he will think that something valuable has crashed and will be upset. Or get angry at the children who left the window open.

T. And what will he do?
P. Probably, he will go and see what the matter is. Of course, he will not call the police.

T. So, as we have seen in this example, the same situation allows for different interpretations. And on how a person interprets the situation, his feelings and behavior depend.

Such sketches allow the patient to explore their thoughts and feelings, distancing themselves from their own problems. However, it is impossible to determine in advance how effective one or another sketch will turn out in each particular case. The therapist should try out various examples and should be ready to build new models based on the experience of the patient himself.

The relationship between thinking and effect can also be demonstrated using the technique of "artificially evoked images." The therapist asks the patient to imagine some unpleasant situation. If an unpleasant image is accompanied by negative emotion, the therapist asks the patient about the content of his thoughts. Then he asks the patient to conjure up some pleasant scene and describe his feelings. Typically, it is not difficult for patients to understand that a person can control his mood by changing the content of his thoughts. This technique is indicated for mild depressive disorders.

Cognition and Recent Experiences

To induce a patient to become aware of their cognitions, sometimes it is enough to ask him about recent experiences, for example, about thoughts that visited him before the first therapeutic session. Many patients admit that they thought about the therapist, the upcoming treatment, and the possible results of therapy. If these thoughts had a negative connotation, the therapist designates them with the term "automatic thoughts" (cognition).

By identifying such experiences, the therapist is able to correct the patient's erroneous ideas about the upcoming treatment. So, one of the patients, in response to a question about what she was thinking while sitting in the waiting room, admitted that she was tormented by the thought that she could not stand such a long therapy. The patient was informed about the total duration of the course of cognitive therapy (weekly hourly sessions for 12-14 weeks); however, this information was contrary to the information received from another consultant who said that she would need to undergo a two- or three-year course of therapy with three sessions in Week. In fact, the patient did not understand that the consultant had in mind a completely different therapeutic system (psychoanalysis), pursuing completely different goals ("complete personality restructuring").

When the patient clarified the difference between cognitive and psychoanalytic therapy, her fears gave way to more relevant doubts ("Will this therapy be successful?", "What if I don't feel better?" etc.).

Identification of Automatic Thoughts

After the patient understands the meaning of the term "cognition" and realizes the presence of automatic thoughts and images, the therapist and patient proceed to the next step - the identification of dysfunctional cognitions.

How exactly these cognitions will be revealed depends on the content of the investigated problem. Typically, the patient is instructed to "catch" and record all the negative thoughts and images that arise from him. The greatest accuracy of reproduction is achieved if the patient writes down each thought immediately after its occurrence. However, in practice, this is not always possible. Therefore, the therapist asks the patient to give 15 minutes each night to lose the events of the last day in his mind and recall the thoughts and experiences associated with them. The patient should reproduce his thoughts as accurately as possible, using direct rather than indirect speech. So, for example, instead of saying: "I thought that I would never become a good engineer," he should write: "I will never become a good engineer."

Another method for collecting cognition is based on the identification of environmental events associated with depression. We illustrate the application of this method with a specific example. A 31-year-old patient, a mother of three, said that the "hardest time" for her is the morning, from 7 to 9, when she picks up the children and feeds them breakfast. The woman could not explain this fact until she began to write down her thoughts. She found that talking with children in the morning; she constantly compares herself with her mother, who, according to her recollections, was always out of sorts in the morning. If the children behaved badly or molested her with different requests, she would say to herself: "Don't be angry. Otherwise, you will push them away from you forever." She tried not to pay attention to the antics and whims of the children, but she often "exploded," and after that, she was tormented by the thought: "I am worse than my mother. I am not able to take care of my own children. It will be better for them if I die." Her negative childhood memories acted even more depressingly on the patient: "I remember how my mother spanked me when I was capricious." Awareness of these cognitions opened the way for a fruitful discussion of the patient's problems, in particular, her beliefs about the inadmissibility of anger when communicating with children.

Depressive cognitions can also be identified as a result of the confrontation of the patient with unpleasant environmental stimuli. A 49-year-old patient who lost her son two years ago (he committed suicide) blamed himself for his death. A lot of objects and situations (kind of guitar, listening to music, visiting the exhibition) reminded her of her son and caused an influx of painful thoughts and feelings of guilt. She tried to avoid situations that could stir up these memories and thereby deprived herself of the opportunity to become aware of her depressive thoughts. The therapist invited the patient to visit the local art gallery and write down all the thoughts that she would have while watching the paintings. As a result, it was found that all her thoughts were self-incriminating. The woman constantly scolded herself for "not finding time to listen to her son," for her inability to break up an unhappy marriage and "parental incompetence." As a result of the subsequent discussion with the therapist, the patient came to the conclusion that her self-incrimination was unfounded.

Another effective technique is that the patient is asked to write down thoughts that revolve around a topic. A 22-year-old patient, a college student, underwent a course of cognitive therapy for six weeks in connection with depression, when the therapist explained to her the need to cancel the next session.

Patient Okay. I understood - you have a meeting. (Pause.) You know, I guess I should tell you. I thought you wanted to get rid of me.

Therapist. What gave you a reason to think so?

P., I don't know. I just thought that if you wanted to, you probably could make time to see me. But I don't even know if you will be in the city.

The therapist asked the patient to pay attention to thoughts revolving around the topic of "rejection." In the next session, the patient said that over the past Week, such thoughts had visited her 27 times. The therapist found out how the patient understood "rejection" and discussed her expectations with others about her (the patient unconsciously believed that others should sacrifice their own interests for her all the time).

As you can see, the task of detecting depressive cognitions of a patient can be solved using various methods. Having learned to identify these cognitions, the patient, together with the therapist, begins to study the sources of depression.

The Study of Automatic Thoughts and Verification of Reality

Encouraging the patient to check the reliability and validity of his ideas, the therapist is far from instilling false optimism in the patient - he only pushes him to a more accurate perception and analysis of the events. Despite the fact that a depressed person does see the world in a gloomy light, the therapist must be careful in his conclusions, because not all pessimistic or nihilistic opinions of the patient are baseless. Any idea should be investigated and tested using generally accepted standards of logical thinking.

The young patient was convinced that the college to which she sent her documents would refuse her admission. A thorough study of the facts showed that the girl's conviction has no real basis.

Therapist. Why do you think that you will not be accepted to this university?

Patient: Because my grades are not so high.

T. What is your average rating?

P. Somewhere between "A" and "B."

T. Which are more - "A" or "B"?

P. Basically "A," but in the last semester, I showed terrible results.

T. And what were your grades in the last semester?

P. Two, "A" and two "B."

T. As I understand it, your average result is closer to level "A." Why do you think you will not go to university?

P. There is too much competition.

T. Did you find out what the passing score is?

P. I was told that the average result should not be lower than the "B +" level.

T. But is your result not higher than this level?

P. Yes, perhaps that is higher.

The patient did not at all try, as it might seem at first glance, to deceive the therapist - she really underestimated her chances of entering the university. We have here an example of absolutist thinking, thinking of the type "all or nothing": any assessment below level "A" was perceived by the girl as a failure. In addition, the patient did not correlate her indicators with the results of other students. Only by carefully considering the factual side of the matter was she able to realize the fallacy of her conclusions.

In this case, it would be possible to apply other approaches, which, perhaps, would have a beneficial effect on the patient, but would hardly teach her to verify the validity of her ideas. Firstly, the therapist could assure the patient that she is smart enough and, therefore, will certainly go to college. Secondly, he could take advantage of the strategy adopted in rational-emotive therapy (Ellis, 1962) and prove to the patient that the mere fact of not going to college does not detract from the merits of a person.

However, if the therapist had resorted to these strategies at this stage of therapy, he would have missed one extremely important point; namely, he would not have collected a solid database to verify the patient's conclusions and would deprive the patient of the opportunity to correlate their conclusions with the facts. Even if the patient felt improvement as a result of the rational-emotive approach, she would have retained her negative cognitive attitude and would subsequently erroneously interpret other situations, and perhaps even return to her previous (erroneous) conclusions about the impossibility of going to college.

As you know, not every applicant has a good certificate, and pessimistic forecasts of a depressed applicant can be justified. If the therapist found that the girl really has no chance of going to college, he would investigate what significance she attaches to this event and would reveal all the prejudices associated with this value. Perhaps he would have received an answer from her: "If I do not go to college, then I am a dumbass," or: "... I will never be happy," or: "Parents will be terribly disappointed." These prejudices are also subject to research on their relevance to reality. If it turns out, for example, that for parents, such an event would really mean disaster, the therapist may ask the patient why she allows herself to depend on their desires and feelings. Thus, the therapist brings the patient to the realization that the person makes himself unhappy, focusing on the opinions and expectations of others. However, as our experience shows, attempts to correct attitudes and subjective meanings do not reach their goal as long as the patient continues to distort reality.

Patient X. complained of severe headaches and other somatic disorders. Beck's survey results showed a deep depression. The following cognitions associated with depression were revealed in the patient: "My family members do not reckon with me," "Nobody pays attention to me," "I am nothingness."

As an example of the inattentive attitude of relatives, the patient named the "fact" that her seventeen-year-old son did not want to spend time with her. Although this statement seemed quite plausible, the therapist decided to make sure that it really was.

Patient He does not want to go to the cinema or to the theater with me.

Therapist. How do you know that he does not want to?

P. Teenagers do not like spending time with their parents.

T. Did you invite him to go to the cinema or to the theater with you?

P. No. On the contrary, he himself asked a couple of times if I wanted to take it with me, but I don't think he really wanted to.

T. Maybe ask him directly?

P. Yes, you can.

T. It is important not that he goes to the cinema or does not go to the cinema with you, but that you ascribe to him some desires or unwillingness instead of finding out from him what he wants.

P. Perhaps you are right. But you know, he is still very inattentive. He, for example, is constantly late for dinner.

T. How many times was he late for dinner?

P. Well, once or twice... No, of course, not always.

T. Is he late for dinner due to the fact that he is an inattentive son?

P. No, I remembered, he said that he had a lot of work. And frankly, in other respects, he is a pretty sensitive boy.

As you can see, the therapist does not accept the patient's statements on faith, but subjects each to a thorough examination. If the patient was found to be right in her conclusions, then the therapist would try to clarify what her son's "carelessness" means.

Depressed patients are inherent in treating their ideas and conclusions as facts. In general, this is common to all people, but with depression, this trend becomes especially pronounced due to the distortion of perception and thinking. The problem is aggravated by the fact that errors in perception and thinking negatively affect the patient's behavior.

When the patient learns to identify and fix his cognitions, he begins to grasp the connection between individual cognitions and painful emotions. The structure and content of each cognition are associated with the resulting effect (Beck, 1976). For example, anxiety is associated with the perception of a threat (physical or social). The cognition associated with depression usually reflects the patient's conviction of his own incompetence, unattractiveness, and inferiority.

Under the guidance of the therapist, the patient learns to classify his cognitions according to the dominant topics (for example, the topic of self-accusation, the topic of inferiority, etc.) and begins to realize the possibility of other, more positive, interpretations and meanings of an event. Using specific examples, the therapist can show the patient that he systematically chooses the most negative interpretations, even when these interpretations are clearly contrary to the facts. Of course, one should not expect that the patient, having realized this tendency, will instantly change his point of view. The latter result can be achieved only by a thorough study of each interpretation with the simultaneous development of patient observation and logical thinking.

The therapist has at his disposal a range of cognitive techniques to evaluate and verify the patient's conclusions. The need to correct stereotypical negative reactions is determined by the fact that they give rise to negative emotions in the patient and prevent him from concentrating on real problems. Among these techniques, the techniques of "re-attribution" and "alternative conceptualization" deserve special mention. Their main advantage is due to the fact that the patient learns to "distance" from his own thoughts; that is, he begins to consider the thought as a psychological phenomenon.

The Technique of Re-Attribution

The cognitive pattern of a depressed patient usually contains an element of self-flagellation. In depression, a person tends to blame himself or take responsibility for the adverse outcome of events, even in those cases when he really could not influence the result. If the therapist discovers that the patient explains the troubles only with his own miscalculations and flaws, for example, scolds himself for his ineptitude or lack of diligence, he can apply the re-attribution technique. The purpose of this technique is not to completely remove the responsibility of the patient, but to highlight all the factors that could affect the outcome of events through an objective analysis of the situation. An objective view of things helps the patient to clarify their miscalculations, and to develop ways to correct an unfavorable situation and prevent its recurrence.

We illustrate the application of this technique by the following example.

The moderately depressed patient, a 52-year-old bank clerk, complained that he could not work "as efficiently as before." Speaking of "inefficiency," he meant that it became difficult for him to make business decisions. In the fourth session, the patient came extremely dejected.

A patient. You can't imagine how I ruined everything! I made another mistake - an unforgivable mistake that can cost me a job.

Therapist. Tell us what the mistake was.

P. I authorized the issuance of a loan to an insolvent borrower. I made the wrong decision again.

T. Do you remember how you made this decision?

P. Yes, of course. On paper, everything looked great: good security, high credit rating. But I had to anticipate that problems would arise.

T. Did you had all the necessary information when you made a decision?

P. No, then no. But after six weeks I had all the information ... You see, they expect to profit from me, and I squander the bank's money.

T. I understand you are upset. But I want to know what kind of information you had at the time of the decision.

When the patient, compelled by the therapist, compared all the data, he came to the conclusion that he acted in accordance with the established rules for granting loans. Using the method of re-attribution allowed the patient to understand that an unpleasant situation arose, not through his fault. However, now, the patient had to solve the problem with the report. The fact is that cursing himself for alleged oversights, he did not report the situation to the leadership. The therapist convinced the patient that it was not too late to correct this error, and helped to develop an acceptable plan of action.

The technique of re-attribution is especially useful when dealing with patients who are prone to self-flagellation and / or assuming excessive responsibility. The therapist can apply the following tactics: a) consider the "facts" that caused self-criticism (as in the case described above); b) show the patient that he proceeds from different criteria in assessing his own behavior and the actions of other people (double standard); c) challenge the patient's conviction that he is "one hundred percent" responsible for the adverse situation.

Search for Alternative Solutions

The limited system of logic and argumentation of a depressed patient becomes more open when the patient distances himself from his own cognitions and begins to identify patterns of his thinking and preservative topics. Problems that previously seemed insoluble can be rethought. At this stage of therapy, beneficial it turns out to be the technique of "alternative conceptualization," the essence of which is reduced to the active study of all possible interpretations and solutions to the problem.

Having defined in detail the essence of his difficulties, the patient can completely spontaneously come to the solution of problems that seemed unsolvable. A fresh, open-minded view of the problem allows the patient to consider a variety of possibilities that previously simply were not taken into account. Usually, a depressed patient sincerely believes that he has investigated all possible approaches to the problem, but in fact, it turns out that some opportunities are missed or rejected by him because of the prejudice of his thinking. The following example illustrates how a negative cognitive attitude forces a person to see an insoluble problem in their difficulties.

A 28-year-old patient, a mother of three children, was desperate that her husband had abandoned her. She did not get tired of repeating that she "would not survive" without him. The woman justified her despair by the fact that she, they say, is not adapted for an independent life. While still a teenager, she was afraid to be alone, and when she got married, she hardly tolerated her husband's business trips. She did not know how to plan a family budget; she did not know how to manage money wisely and was afraid that children would become a victim of her impracticality. According to her, with the departure of her husband, life turned for her into a "nightmare."

The first step to using the "alternative conceptualization" technique was to identify the patient's problems (cost management, the discipline of children, loneliness). Each of these problems terrified the patient since, in the past, she had never managed to cope with them. The woman said: "I was never strong in mathematics," "Jack was always involved in discipline issues," "I was always afraid to be alone - what if something happens?"

Perhaps this was the case in the past, but at the moment, the patient faced the problem of acquiring specific skills that would allow her to lead an independent life. As it turned out, the patient had a college diploma; the woman admitted that deep down, she did not like to depend on her husband completely. Later it turned out that the patient is able to find a way out of a difficult situation. For example, she found out about loan programs for the population and began to think about looking for a secretary. After a joint study of these possibilities, the therapist returned to discussing the patient's initial opinion that she "would not survive" without her husband. By this time, the patient's mood had improved markedly, and she decided to try to realize one of the possibilities in order to improve her financial situation. She managed to get a bank loan; the success of this initiative inspired the patient and refuted her initial belief in her own incompetence.

It should be noted that the "search for solutions" often causes significant shifts in the patient's mood. This change of mood is explained by the sudden realization that the situation is not as hopeless as it seemed before. However, the task of the therapist is not limited to, considering alternative approaches to the problem. He should also help the patient objectively analyze his previous conclusions (for example: "I never succeed"). No matter how unlikely such conclusions may seem, they seem very plausible to a depressed patient, and, as a rule, he finds a lot of "convincing" evidence of his own incompetence and ineptitude. The patient cannot suddenly abandon his conviction; he needs time to integrate a new point of view ("I have certain knowledge, but I have to acquire some practical skills"). The search for alternative approaches is an important point in the treatment of suicidal patients (see chapter 10).

By comprehending alternative explanations, the patient overcomes his preconceptions and learns to form more accurate judgments. A change in thinking leads to positive changes in the mood and behavior of the patient. We illustrate this point with a concrete example.

The patient, a 22-year-old college student, was convinced that the English teacher considered her "incapable." To confirm this conclusion, she showed the therapist a copy of her essay. The work earned the mark "C" and was accompanied by two pages of criticisms, which plunged the girl into despair. She saw this as evidence of her "inability" and was ready to drop out of college.

During the discussion, it turned out that the patient was writing an essay, already in a state of depression, and therefore it was logical to assume that the results of her work do not reflect her true abilities. Even the patient herself, recalling her work on the essay, was surprised that she even managed to write it. It is clear that in the context of this information, the low grade and criticisms of the professor looked somewhat different. However, priority the therapist's task was to help the patient explore her opinion of her own "inability."

The therapist asked the girl to give all possible explanations and then rank them according to the degree of "credibility." The list of explanations compiled by the patient looked like this.

1. "I am not capable of languages" - 90%.

2. "The professor is biased towards girls" - 5%.

3. "My grade is not very different from the ratings of other students" - 3%.

4. "The professor commented, wanting to help me. So, he does not consider me hopeless"- 2%.

The therapist managed to persuade the girl to call the professor directly from his office ("Either now or never") and find out how he assesses her prospects. As a result of the conversation, it turned out that 1) the average rating for the group did not exceed the level "C" and that, 2) despite the claims to the style, the professor liked the content of the essay. The professor invited the student to meet to discuss his comments in detail. After this telephone conversation, the girl looked lively and enthusiastic. The previous despair about their own "inability" was replaced by a desire and willingness to work on improving their style, and the thought of quitting college gave way to a decision to take several private lessons.

This case clearly shows how a negative interpretation of events can affect a person's emotional state and behavior. Not in itself, the fact of receiving a low rating, but the interpretation of this event led the patient into despair. The girl not only became discouraged but also was going to act on the basis of her negative conclusions. Clearly, she would have made a big mistake if she dropped out; a similar outcome of events would be for her another proof of her imaginary inability. It was the study of all possible interpretations that led the patient to a more reasonable, more constructive solution.

The identification and ranking of cognitions allowed the therapist and patient to formulate working hypotheses that could be empirically verified. At the end of the session, the patient re-evaluated her interpretations for reliability and realized that she overestimated the reliability of the first hypothesis due to a lack of objective information. It should be noted that the professor's explanations helped shift the emphasis from the fact of failure to the fact of the absence of certain skills: the girl ceased to consider herself "incapable," but thought about the need to improve her style.

In this case, the patient received the missing information without leaving the therapist's office. In cases where this is not possible, the patient should be given "urgent homework," namely, instructed to collect the necessary information as soon as possible and then immediately contact the therapist. The urgency is due to the fact that the patient can extend his negative conclusions to other situations. In some cases, it is useful to attract "significant others" - friends or relatives of the patient.

The Protocol of Dysfunctional Thoughts

A technique for recording dysfunctional thoughts is also used to identify, study, and correct cognitions. The patient is given a form consisting of two or more columns. In one column, the patient should write down the automatic thoughts that arise in him, and in the other - "reasonable answers" to these thoughts. In additional columns, the patient can note his reaction (affective or behavioral) to these thoughts, as well as describe the situation or event that preceded cognition. The standard form of the "Protocol of dysfunctional thoughts" includes the following columns: "Date", "Situation", "Emotions", "Automatic Thoughts", "Rational Answer", "Result" (see Appendix).

The therapist must explain to the patient how to use the form and give examples of automatic thoughts. The patient should also be taught to evaluate the degree of emotional intensity and the likelihood of negative cognitions; the last condition is dictated by the fact that the patient should write down even those thoughts that seem to him to be "alien" (unlikely). In addition, it allows you to quantify the positive changes that occur in the emotional state and thinking of the patient.

The main task of the therapist is to help the patient find reasonable answers to negative cognitions. Registration of negative thoughts allows the patient to distance themselves from them, and then, together with the therapist, objectively examine them. During the study, the patient begins to understand how negative cognition affects emotions and behavior, and, most importantly, learns a more realistic interpretation of events.

The therapist is free to change the names of the columns according to the needs of the patient. The following two protocols are a modified version of the technique.

A patient, a medical archivist with a 6-year "experience" of depression

Event Feelings Thoughts Other Possible Interpretations

The nurse from the cardiology department was rude to me when I asked her to fill out an appointment sheet for the upcoming commission. She said: "I hate these appointment sheets." Bitterness.

Mild irritation.

Feeling of loneliness

She doesn't love me

This lady is always out of sorts. Just because she hates appointment sheets doesn't mean she hates me — she just doesn't like paperwork. She has a lot of work, and she was in a hurry. It is foolish to relate to the appointment sheets; they are her only defense in the event of a lawsuit.

The patient, a 24-year-old nurse, was recently discharged from the clinic.

Event Feelings Thoughts Other Possible Interpretations

When I was discharged from the hospital, my friends invited me to a party. There Jim came up to me. He asked, "How are you feeling?" Anxiety Jim considers me seriously ill. Do I really look so bad that he finds it necessary to inquire about my well-being?

I am not indifferent to him. He noticed that I look better than before, and therefore asked about my well-being.

Conclusion

Efficiency

It is important to note that the movement of behavioral therapy has brought with it a series of techniques that were shorter and apparently more effective. The endless number of 50-minute psychotherapy sessions is replaced by a much shorter series of consultations that focus on patient complaints. The endless discovery of the underlying pathology, the comprehensive classification of the patient's history, and the long insight search are eliminated.

A Set of Techniques

Behavioral therapy has evolved to a wide range of techniques ranging from systematic desensitization to cognitive restructuring. In order to increase the likelihood of the right decision being made, the therapist is likely to gather the information that best matches the technique suitable for the patient.

Technology

Behavioral therapy is a very active set of procedures. It involves evaluation, planning, decisions, and techniques and, in a way, can be considered with complex technology. You cannot passively assign a technology to a patient; it is something that must be guided by care and prediction and with great attention to detail. If a therapist uses aggressive procedures, the temporary relationship to the stimulus outbreak and the outbreak of punishment may need strict supervision. This lively and vigorous quality that behavioral methods and the analogous activity that this entails in the therapist are responsible for some improvement in the patient beyond that caused by the specific procedure used.

References

1. Beck, A. T., and B. F. Shaw. 1977. Cognitive approaches to depression. In Vol. 1 of Handbook of Rational Emotive Therapy, edited by A. Ellis and R. Grieger, 119–134. New York: Springer.

2. Beers, C. 1908. A Mind That Found Itself. New York: Longmans and Green.

3. Beevers, C. G., and I. W. Miller. 2005. Unlinking negative cognition and symptoms of depression: Evidence of a specific treatment effect for cognitive therapy. Journal of Consulting and Clinical Psychology 73: 68–77.

4. Benazzi, F. 2003. Anger in bipolar depression. Journal of Clinical Psychiatry 64: 480–481.

5. Berne, E. 1964. Games People Play: The Psychology of Human Relations. New York: Grove Press.

6. Braverman, E. 2004. Balanced Brain Advantage: The Edge Effect. New York: Sterling.

7. Bruder, G. E., J. W. Stew art, P. J. McGrath, G. J. Ma Guoguang, B. E. Wexler, and F. M.

8. Quitkin. 2002. A typical depression: Enhanced right hemispheric dominance for perceiving emotional chimeric faces. Journal of Abnormal Psychology 111 (3): 446–454.

9. Burns, D. D. 1999. Feeling Good. New York: Avon Books.

10. Burns, D. D., and S. Nolen-Hoeksema. 1991. Coping styles, homework compliance, and the effectiveness of cognitive-behavioral therapy. Journal of Consulting and Clinical Psychology 59: 305–311.

11. Burton, R. 2001. The Anatomy of Melancholy. New York: Review Books Classic.

12. Cart wright, R., M. A. Young, P. Mercer, and M. Bears. 1998. Role of REM sleep and dream variables in the pre diction of remission from depression. Psychiatry Research 21: 249–255.

13. Cooley, C. H. 1902. Human Nature and the Social Order. New York: Scribner.

14. Cox, B. J., and M. W. Enns. 2003. Relative stability of perfection in depression. Canadian Journal of Behavioral Science 35 (2): 124–132.

15. Barlow, D. H. 2004. Improving outcomes in patients with generalized anxiety disorder and panic disorder: Role of

psychological treatments. CNS Spectrums 9 (11 Suppl. 13): 1–8.

16. Beck, A. T., and B. F. Shaw. 1977. Cognitive approaches to depression. In Vol. 1 of Handbook of Rational Emotive Therapy, edited by A. Ellis and R. Grieger, 119–134. New York: Springer.

17. Beers, C. 1908. A Mind That Found Itself. New York: Longmans and Green.

18. Benazzi, F. 2003. Anger in bipolar depression. Journal of Clinical Psychiatry 64: 480–481. Berne, E. 1964. Games People Play: The Psychology of Human Relations.

19. New York: Grove Press. Braverman, E. 2004. Balanced Brain Advantage: The Edge Effect. New York: Sterling.

20. Bruder, G. E., J. W. Stewart, P. J. McGrath, G. J. Ma Guoguang, B. E. Wexler, and F. M.

21. Quitkin. 2002. Atypical depression: Enhanced right hemispheric dominance for perceiving emotional chimeric faces. Journal of Abnormal Psychology 111 (3): 446–454.

22. Burns, D. D. 1999. Feeling Good. New York: Avon Books.

23. Burns, D. D., and S. Nolen-Hoeksema. 1991. Coping styles, homework compliance, and the effectiveness of cognitive-behavioral therapy. Journal of Consulting and Clinical Psychology 59: 305–311.

24. Burton, R. 2001. The Anatomy of Melancholy. New York: Review Books Classic.

25. Cartwright, R., M. A. Young, P. Mercer, and M. Bears. 1998. Role of REM sleep and dream variables in the prediction of remission from depression. Psychiatry Research 21: 249–255.

26. Cooley, C. H. 1902. Human Nature and the Social Order. New York: Scribner.

27. Cox, B. J., and M. W. Enns. 2003. Relative stability of perfection in depression. Canadian Journal of Behavioral Science 35 (2): 124–132.

28. Cox, D. L., S. D. Stabb, and J. F. Hulgus. 2000. Anger and depression in girls and boys: A study of gender differences. Psychology of Women Quarterly 24: 110–112.